SCOTLAND'S NEW WRITING THEATRE

Traverse Theatre Company

The People Next Door

by Henry Adam

Cast in order of appearance

Nigel	Fraser Ayres
Marco	Jimmy Akingbola
Phil	Joe Duttine
Mrs Mac	Eileen McCallum

Director	Roxana Silbert
Designer	Miriam Buether
Lighting Designer	Neil Austin
Sound Designer	Matt McKenzie
Fight Director	Terry King
Stage Manager	Lee Davies
Deputy Stage Manager	Victoria Paulo
Assistant Stage Manager	Kenna Grant
Casting Consultant	Amy Ball
Casting Assistant	Neil Coull

**First performed at the Traverse Theatre
Friday 11 July 2003**

TRAVERSE THEATRE

powerhouse of new writing DAILY TELEGRAPH

Artistic Director Philip Howard

The Traverse is Scotland's new writing theatre. Founded in 1963 by a group of maverick artists and enthusiasts, it began as an imaginative attempt to capture the spirit of adventure and experimentation of the Edinburgh Festival all year round. Throughout the decades, the Traverse has evolved and grown in artistic output and ambition. It has refined its mission by strengthening its commitment to producing new plays by Scottish and international playwrights and actively nurturing them throughout their careers. Traverse productions have been seen worldwide and tour regularly throughout the UK and overseas.

The Traverse has produced over 600 new plays in its lifetime and, through a spirit of innovation and risk-taking, has launched the careers of many of the country's best known writers. From, among others, Stanley Eveling in the 1960s, John Byrne in the 1970s, Liz Lochhead in the 1980s, to David Greig and David Harrower in the 1990s, the Traverse is unique in Scotland in its dedication to new writing. It fulfils the crucial role of providing the infrastructure, professional support and expertise to ensure the development of a dynamic theatre culture for Scotland.

The Traverse's activities encompass every aspect of playwriting and production, providing and facilitating play reading panels, script development workshops, rehearsed readings, public playwriting workshops, writers' groups, a public playwrights' platform, The Monday Lizard, discussions and special events. The Traverse's work with young people is of supreme importance and takes the form of encouraging playwriting through its flagship education project, Class Act, as well as the Traverse Young Writers Group.

Edinburgh's Traverse Theatre is a mini-festival in itself THE TIMES

From its conception in the 1960s, the Traverse has remained a pivotal venue during the Edinburgh Festival. It receives enormous critical and audience acclaim for its programming, as well as regularly winning awards. In 2001 the Traverse was awarded two Scotsman Fringe Firsts and two Herald Angels for its own productions of *Gagarin Way* and *Wiping My Mother's Arse* and a Herald Archangel for overall artistic excellence. In 2002 the Traverse again had the pick of the Fringe Festival productions with *Outlying Islands* and *Iron* winning awards and transferring to the Royal Court Theatre, London. During the year the Traverse also reinforced its international profile and touring activities with a European tour of *Gagarin Way* and a successful Highlands & Islands tour of *Homers*.

For further information on the Traverse Theatre's activities and history, an online resource is available at www.virtualtraverse.co.uk. To find out about ways to support the Traverse, please contact Norman MacLeod, Development Manager, on 0131 228 3223.

COMPANY BIOGRAPHIES

Henry Adam (Writer): Henry was born in Wick, Caithness. His first full length play for the Traverse, AMONG UNBROKEN HEARTS, transferred to The Bush Theatre, London in May 2001 after successful runs in Edinburgh and the Highlands. AMONG UNBROKEN HEARTS was joint winner of the 2002 Meyer Whitworth Award. Other previous plays include: AN CLO MOR (Theatre Highland); MILLENNIUM-ANGELS OF PARIS (His Majesties, Aberdeen); THE WIDOW (Sharp Shorts, Traverse Theatre); THE ABATTOIR (winner Mobil Scottish Playwriting Competition).

Neil Austin (Lighting Designer): For the Traverse: MR PLACEBO (co-production with Drum Theatre Royal, Plymouth). Other theatre includes: A PRAYER FOR OWEN MEANY, THE WALLS, FURTHER THAN THE FURTHEST THING (National Theatre); CALIGULA (Donmar Warehouse); JAPES (Theatre Royal, Haymarket); FLESH WOUND, TRUST (Royal Court); CUCKOOS (BITE-Pit,Barbican); MONKEY (Young Vic); AMERICAN BUFFALO (Royal Exchange, Manchester); WORLD MUSIC, THE MODERNISTS (Sheffield Crucible); THE LADY IN THE VAN, PRETENDING TO BE ME (West Yorkshire Playhouse); GREAT EXPECTATIONS (Bristol Old Vic); KING HEDLEY II (Birmingham Rep & Tricycle); ROMEO & JULIET, TWELFTH NIGHT (Liverpool Playhouse); LOVES WORK, CUCKOOS, VENECIA (Gate Theatre); CLOSER (Teatro Broadway, Buenos Aires). Musicals include: BABES IN ARMS (Cardiff International Festival of Musical Theatre); SPEND, SPEND, SPEND (UK Tour - co-design with Mark Henderson); MY FAIR LADY (Teatro Nacional, Buenos Aires); BONNIE & CLYDE (Guildhall). Operas include: THE EMBALMER (Almeida Opera); ORFEO (Opera City, Tokyo); PULSE SHADOWS (Queen Elizabeth Hall); L'ENFANT PRODIGUE, LE PORTRAIT DE MANON (Guildhall).

Fraser Ayres (*Nigel*): Theatre includes: RAMAYANA (National Theatre); RAMPAGE, FOUR AND BLUEBIRD (Royal Court); VURT ("Scribble" Contact Theatre); TELLING TALES (Lyric Hammersmith); THE LOVES OF LADY PURPLE, SANDMAN (Leicester Haymarket and National Theatre). Film includes: REVENGERS TRAGEDY, INTIMACY, IT WAS AN ACCIDENT, RAGE, SPEAK LIKE A CHILD, DINNER FOR TWO, JUST ONE KISS, KEVIN AND PERRY. Television includes: UNCONDITIONAL LOVE, DOGMA TV, TRAIL OF GUILT, THE BILL, THE VICE, URBAN GOTHIC, SWIVEL ON THE TIP, UNTO THE WICKED, LONDON'S BURNING.

Jimmy Akingbola (*Marco*): Theatre includes: PLAYING FIELDS (Soho, London); NAKED JUSTICE (West Yorkshire Playhouse); BABY DOLL (National Theatre/Albery Theatre); THE CHANGELING

(National Theatre/Studio); NATIVITY (Birmingham Rep); RAMAYANA (Birmingham Rep/National Theatre); READY OR NOT RAW (Theatre Royal, Stratford). TV includes: THE CROUCHES, ROGER ROGER, DOCTORS (BBC); THE SLIGHTLY FILTHY SHOW (Carlton); THE SOUTH BANK SHOW (LWT). Film includes: ANANSI (Avista Films) and THE DIMPLES CRY. Radio includes: THE FIRE CHILDREN (BBC Radio 3); A NOISE IN THE NIGHT, CLOTHES OF NAKEDNESS, WESTWAY, TRINIDAD SISTERS (BBC World Service); DANCING BACKWARDS (BBC Radio 4).

Miriam Buether (Designer): Theatre includes: RED DEMON (Young Vic); BINTOU, ROSENCRANTZ AND GUILDENSTERN ARE DEAD (Arcola Theatre); ESKIMO SISTERS (Southwark Playhouse); LEBENSSPIELE (Three Mills Island Studios, London); ATTEMPTS ON HER LIFE (George Wood Theatre); MIT UNS LEBEN (Parabolica Spaces, Berlin); THE BESPOKE OVERCOAT & THE HEBREW LESSON (New End Theatre, London). Dance includes: TENDER HOOKS (Fundação Calouste Gulbenkian, Lisbon); POSSIBLY SIX (Grand Ballets de Canadiens, Theatre Maisonneuve, Montreal); 7 DS (Rambert Dance Company, Sadler's Wells); EUROVISION YOUNG DANCERS COMPETITION (BBC). Forthcoming: BODY OF POETRY (Komische Oper, Berlin). Film includes: CALENDAR GIRLS (London, Short Film Festival Munich); FAMOUS LAST WORDS (London). Exhibitions/Art-Installations include: set and costume designs for 7 DS (National Theatre); LAZY BOYS AND BUSY BODIES (KX Gallery, Kampnagel Hamburg); GEDANKENGEBAUDE IN DER KUNST (Kunsthaus Hamburg); ARCHITEKTURKLEIDER (National Gallery Sopot, Poland). Awards include Linbury Prize for Stage Design 1999.

Joe Duttine (*Phil*): Theatre includes: PONDLIFE (Bush Theatre); A MONTH IN THE COUNTRY (Palace Theatre, Watford); MY NIGHT WITH REG (Royal Court/Criterion); SWEETHEART (Royal Court); LITTLE MALCOLM & HIS STRUGGLE AGAINST THE EUNUCHS (Hampstead Theatre); THE MYSTERIES (National Theatre). Television includes: THE RED AND THE BLACK, SEAFORTH, PIE IN THE SKY, MY NIGHT WITH REG, SILENT WITNESS, TRUE TILDA, THE BEGGAR BRIDE, DAZIEL AND PASCOE, LOVE IN THE 21ST CENTURY, INSPECTOR LINLEY MYSTERIES (BBC); CAPITAL LIVES (Carlton); BARE NECESSITIES, THE CRY (Granada); SERIOUS & ORGANISED (Company Television). Film includes: THE SWORDS (Showtime); GREENWICH MEANTIME (Greenwich Films); THE NAVIGATORS (Parallax, dir Ken Loach).

Terry King (Fight Director): For the Traverse: IRON, GAGARIN WAY. For the National Theatre: FOOL FOR LOVE (Peter Gill), KING LEAR (David Hare), OTHELLO (Sam Mendes), HENRY V (Nick Hytner), LONDON CUCKOLDS (Terry Johnson), TING TANG MINE (Michael Rudman), DUCHESS OF MALFI (Phillida Lloyd), JERRY SPRINGER THE OPERA (Stewart Lee), ELMINAS KITCHEN (Angus Jackson), EDMUND (Edward Hall). For the RSC: TROILUS AND CRESSIDA (Sam Mendes), ROMEO AND JULIET, CYMBELINE (Adrian Noble), PERICLES (David Thacker), TWELFTH NIGHT (Ian Judge), HENRY IV Pts 1 & 2 (Michael Attenbourgh), HENRY VI Pts 1, 2 & 3 (Michael Boyd), MACBETH (Greg Doran), THE JACOBEAN SEASON (Swan), CORIOLANUS (David Farr). For the Royal Court: THE RECRUITING OFFICER (Max Stafford-Clark), SEARCH AND DESTROY (Stephen Daldry), ASHES AND SAND (Ian Rickson), OLEANNA (Harold Pinter), BERLIN BERTIE (Danny Boyle), GREENLAND (Simon Curtis). Other theatre includes: CALIGULA, ACCIDENTAL DEATH OF AN ANARCHIST (Donmar); LYSISTRATA (Old Vic); DEATH OF A SALESMAN (Bristol); OF MICE AND MEN (Nottingham). Opera and musicals include: PORGY AND BESS (Trevor Nunn); OTELLO (Peter Stein); JESUS CHRIST SUPERSTAR (Gael Edwards); SATURDAY NIGHT FEVER (Arlene Philips); CHITTY CHITTY BANG BANG (Adrian Noble). Work for television includes: THE BILL, CASUALTY, EASTENDERS, BROKEN GLASS, A KIND OF INNOCENCE, FATAL INVERSION, THE MAYOR OF CASTERBRIDGE, LUCKY JIM, ROCKFACE.

Eileen McCallum (*Mrs Mac*): For the Traverse: OLGA. Other theatre work includes: CAT ON A HOT TIN ROOF, PARKING LOT IN PITTSBURGH, A PASSIONATE WOMAN (Byre Theatre); ROMEO AND JULIET (Royal Shakespeare Company); CINDERELLA, MOTHER GOOSE (Kings Theatre, Glasgow); THERESE RAQUIN (Communicado); ALBERTINE IN 5 TIMES (Clyde Unity); SLEEPING BEAUTY (Adam Smith, Kircaldy); THE TRICK IS TO KEEP BREATHING, DUMBSTRUCK (Tron Theatre); IF ONLY…, LAVENDER BLUE, WILLIE ROUGH, THE MISER, ON GOLDEN POND, THE SLAB BOYS, THE SEAL WIFE (Royal Lyceum); GOING FOR A LOVE SONG – One Woman Show (Edinburgh Festival). TV work includes: THE STALKERS APPRENTICE, BLUE CHRISTMAS, DR FINLAY, TAGGART, HOGMANAY SHOWS, THE STEAMIE, HIGH ROAD (STV); CASUALTY, STILL GAME, GEORGE ORWELL STORY, WHITE BIRD PASSES, JUST A BOYS GAME, GREY GRANITE (BBC). Film work includes: A SMALL DEPOSIT (Brassneck Productions); MY LIFE SO FAR (Enigma); SAVED (Newfoundland).

Matt McKenzie (Sound Designer): Previous productions for the Traverse: IRON (also Royal Court, 2002/3). Since joining Autograph in 1984: VERTIGO (Guildford); SATURDAY, SUNDAY, MONDAY, EASY VIRTUE (Chichester, Soho Theatre); FRAME312 (Donmar); MADE IN BANGKOK, THE HOUSE OF BERNARDA ALBA, JOURNEY'S END, A MADHOUSE IN GOA, GASPING, MISERY, MURDER IS EASY, THE ODD COUPLE, PYGMALION, THINGS WE DO FOR LOVE, LONG DAY'S JOURNEY INTO NIGHT, MACBETH (West End); LYSISTRATA, SCHOOL FOR WIVES, MIND MILLIE FOR ME, A STREETCAR NAMED DESIRE, AMADEUS (West End and Broadway), SEXUAL PERVERSITY IN CHICAGO (for Sir Peter Hall); FAMILY REUNION, HENRY V, THE DUCHESS OF MAFLI, HAMLET, THE LIEUTENANT OF INISHMORE, JULIUS CAESAR (RSC). Peter Hall Seasons at The Old Vic and The Piccadilly and designed the sound for: WASTE, CLOUD 9, THE SEAGULL, THE PROVOK'D WIFE, KING LEAR, THE MISANTHROPE, MAJOR BARBARA, FILUMENA, KAFKA'S DICK. Musical work includes: TALK OF THE STEAMIE (Greenwich); LOVE OFF THE SHELF (Nuffield Theatre); FORBIDDEN BROADWAY, BLUES IN THE NIGHT, TANGO ARGENTINO (West End); CAR MAN (West End and International Tour).

Roxana Silbert (Director): Currently Literary Director of the Traverse, previously Associate Director at the Royal Court Theatre and the West Yorkshire Playhouse. For the Traverse: 15 SECONDS, IRON (also Royal Court), GREEN FIELD, QUARTZ. For the Royal Court: BEEN SO LONG, FAIRGAME, BAZAAR, SWEETHEART, ESSEX GIRLS, MULES, WOUNDS TO HER FACE, VOICES FOR NINE (Barclays New Stages) and Artistic Director of COMING ON STRONG (Young Writers Festival 1994). Roxana has also directed THE FAST SHOW LIVE (Phil McIntyre Productions at the Apollo Hammersmith and National Tour); PRECIOUS (West Yorkshire Playhouse); SPLASH HATCH ON THE E GOING DOWN (Donmar Warehouse); CADILLAC RANCH (Soho Theatre); A SERVANT OF TWO MASTERS (Sheffield Crucible); TRANSLATIONS, TOP GIRLS (New Vic); THE PRICE (Bolton Octagon); LOVE (London Opera festival); TWO HORSEMEN (Bush Theatre/Gate Theatre – Winner of Time Out Award); THE LOVERS (Gate); THE TREATMENT (Intercity Festival, Florence); BACKSTROKE IN A CROWDED POOL (National Theatre Pakistan/British Council). Television includes: THE FAST SHOW LIVE (BBC); OPERA LOVERS, APHRODISIAC (World Productions). Radio includes: A DAY IN THE LIFE OF A HUMBLE BEE (BBC R4); THE TALL ONE.

SPONSORSHIP

Sponsorship income enables the Traverse to commission
and produce new plays and to offer audiences a diverse and
exciting programme of events throughout the year

We would like to thank the following companies
for their support throughout the year

CORPORATE SPONSORS

B B C Scotland

BANK OF
SCOTLAND

navyblue

fine and country wines

Canon

pinnacle
communications ltd

NICHOLAS
GROVES
RAINES
ARCHITECTS

CHAMPAGNE
ALAIN THIENOT
REIMS - FRANCE

ANNIVERSARY ANGELS

edNET
internetworkingsolutions

BENNETT & ROBERTSON LLP

People & Projects

Jean McGhee
RECRUITMENT

projects limited

New Horizons
Computer Learning Centers
Scotland

This theatre has the support of the Pearson Playwright's Scheme sponsored by Pearson plc

The Traverse Trivia Quiz in association with Tennents

With thanks to

Stewarts, printers for the Traverse.
Douglas Hall of IMPact Human Resourcing
for management advice arranged through
the Arts & Business skills bank.
Thanks to Claire Aitken of Royal Bank of Scotland
for mentoring support arranged through
the Arts & Business Mentoring Scheme.
Purchase of the Traverse Box Office, computer network
and technical and training equipment
has been made possible with money from
The Scottish Arts Council National Lottery Fund.

Scottish
Arts Council
LOTTERY FUNDED

**The Traverse Theatre's work
would not be possible without the support of**

Scottish
Arts Council

·EDINBVRGH·
THE CITY OF EDINBURGH COUNCIL

The Traverse Theatre receives financial assistance from

The Calouste Gulbenkian Foundation, The Peggy Ramsay
Foundation, The Binks Trust, The Bulldog Prinsep Theatrical Fund,
The Esmée Fairbairn Foundation, The Gordon Fraser Charitable
Trust, The Garfield Weston Foundation, The Paul Hamlyn
Foundation, The Craignish Trust, Lindsay's Charitable Trust,
The Tay Charitable Trust, The Ernest Cook Trust, The Wellcome Trust,
The Sir John Fisher Foundation, The Ruben and Elisabeth Rausing
Trust, The Equity Trust Fund, The Cross Trust, N Smith Charitable
Settlement, Douglas Heath Eves Charitable Trust, The Bill and
Margaret Nicol Charitable Trust, The Emile Littler Foundation,
Mrs M Guido's Charitable Trust, Gouvernement du Québec,
The Canadian High Commission

Charity No. SC002368

**Henry Adam would like to thank Linda Mclean
for her help in the development of this play.**

For their generous help on
THE PEOPLE NEXT DOOR
the Traverse would like to thank

Robin Sutcliffe at Sutcliffe Play UK
Alan Jeffries at Avalon Armory
Dan and all at the Royal Lyceum Theatre
Brian Jarrett and John McPhearson
at Angus / Arbroath Council
Martin Higgins at Comet Electrical
All the staff at Grindlay Court

Sets, props and costumes for
THE PEOPLE NEXT DOOR
created by Traverse Workshops
(funded by the National Lottery)

Scottish
Arts Council
LOTTERY FUNDED

Production photography by Douglas Robertson
Print photography by Euan Myles

**For their continued generous support
of Traverse productions the Traverse thanks**

Habitat

Marks and Spencer, Princes Street

Camerabase

BHS

TRAVERSE THEATRE – THE COMPANY

www.traverse.co.uk • www.virtualtraverse.co.uk

THE PEOPLE NEXT DOOR

Henry Adam

'God's name got taken in vain a lot that morning'
Art Spiegelman
In the Shadow of No Towers

Characters

NIGEL

MRS MAC

PHIL

MARCO

1.

A small housing association flat in modern-day Britain, not the tidiest place in the world. NIGEL BRUNSWICK *is sitting in his comfy chair smoking drugs off a piece of tin foil. There is a mirror close to the side of his chair which acts as company for* NIGEL *when he is stoned and alone. It is safe to say that* NIGEL *and his mirror have had many long, soul-searching conversations late into many a night.* NIGEL *is a big lanky man of mixed, indeterminate race. He is scruffy and unkempt, looking older than he is, which is just the wrong side of twenty five. There is an aura of grunge about* NIGEL, *as if the hippy convoy drove off one night and left him sitting in this chair. By the side of his chair is a Tesco's bag containing a few items of groceries that he might have meant to put away at one point but inevitably forgot. As the lights come up he is smoking, regarding himself in his mirror.*

NIGEL. My name is Salif. Salif, bwa. That' my name. Salif. That' an African name bwa, Moslem name. Salif, meaning ' . . . ??', well, I don't know what it mean but that' be my name now bwa. Salif. Oh sure, you saying – I know you. That ain't no Salify bwa. I went to school with that bwa. That bwa his name be Nigel. Nah, nah, nah, nah, see – my name ain't Nigel. My name Salif. And now Salif is hungry. Salif is gonna make his self some – (*He digs in Tesco bag and pulls out a tin of Campbell's Cream of Tomato soup. He looks quizzically at the soup.*) – soup? Soup? Yeah bwa, soup. Why not? This be famous soup, bwa. This soup 'as 'ad its picture painted.

This ain't no Nigel soup, bwa. This be Salif soup. Soup that's fit for a king.

NIGEL *gets up to put on his soup but is so stoned he has to correct his balance on standing up.*

Now then, where that kitchen go?

Remembering where the kitchen is – it's attached to the living room, the same room really – NIGEL *goes to heat up his soup. A knock comes to the door.*

Oh what? Bwa can't even have hi' soup in peace.

The knock again.

A'right, a'right, I's coming. No need to get yo' little panties all scrunch up.

This cracks NIGEL *up. He stands laughing at what he said. The knock comes again.* NIGEL *goes to the door. He leans into the spy hole, apparently listening to it rather than looking through.*

Who there?

An old woman's voice comes through, frail, with a distinctive Scottish burr. This is MRS McCALLUM.

MRS MAC. Nigel? Are you in there?

NIGEL *curses under his breath, cartoon style, then opens the door a crack.*

NIGEL. Mrs McCallum. And how are you today?

MRS MAC. Somebody has been smoking in the stair.

NIGEL. I'm sorry. I mean – wha'?

MRS MAC. Somebody has been smoking in the stair.

NIGEL (*taking look outside, left and right*). What you mean? 'Somebody been smoking in the stair'?

MRS MAC. Just what I say. Somebody's been smoking in the stair. I found this. Look. (*She brandishes a dog end, allowing* NIGEL *plenty of time to inspect it.*) Now, I don't mind smoking, Nigel, as well you know – I'm quite partial to the odd puff myself – but this is a nice stair, and we want to keep it that way. How can we keep it nice if people keep throwing their fag ends all over it. It makes a mockery of the entire cleaning process.

NIGEL. Ah, wait. Wait, wait, wait. Not guilty, see.

MRS MAC. Now nobody's accusing anybody of anything Nigel, it's just . . .

NIGEL *runs inside to his ashtray and fishes out one of his own dog ends. He runs back, brandishing it.*

NIGEL. Not guilty. See . . . Look.

MRS MAC. Look at what, Nigel?

NIGEL. At this. Look at this.

MRS MAC *inspects what he is holding up.*

MRS MAC. What is it? Oh. You roll your own.

NIGEL. Yes, Mrs McCallum, I do. I do roll my own.

MRS MAC. And you never . . .

NIGEL. No, Mrs McCallum, I never.

MRS MAC. So it can't have been . . .

NIGEL. That's what I'm saying Mrs McCallum. It can't have been me. Not guilty see. Not me.

MRS MAC *looks a little downhearted.*

Hey, but listen . . . I'll look out for him, eh? Whoever he is. I see anybody smoking round here I'll tell them.

MRS MAC. I'm not fussing, Nigel. It's just such a nice stair. We want to keep it that way.

NIGEL. That's exactly what I'll tell him, Mrs McCallum. Nice stair. Keep it, yeah?

MRS MAC. Oh well. Time for tea I suppose. Is it soup you're having?

NIGEL. What? Yeah. Soup. Campbell's Cream of Tomato. It's 'ad its picture painted.

MRS MAC. I'm partial to a bit of soup myself, especially in this weather. Terrible the weather we've been having lately, isn't it?

NIGEL. Isn't it though? (*His fingers imitate raindrops falling on his head.*) Rain, rain, rain.

MRS MAC. Still, good for the tatties I should imagine.

NIGEL. Good for the . . . ? Yeah, okay Mrs McCallum. I'll be seeing you now. Take care.

MRS MAC. Bye Nigel. And just you remember . . .

NIGEL. Yeah. Nice stair, keep it that way. Got it.

NIGEL *finally gets the door shut. He puts his back against it to bar any further intruders. He smiles and punches the air, then begins to strut.*

Hah! Not guilty. Not guilty, see. You don't get me so easy, Mrs Mac. Roll-ups, see. Me only smoke roll-ups. That there evidence you got there, that be made in some factory, see. Do I look like a factory? Do I? These are what I smoke. These. No logos see, no logos. Hah! (*Confused pause.*) Okay. So what's me doing? Soup, yeah.

NIGEL *goes into the kitchen area to heat up his soup. A knock comes to the door.*

Ah what? What now? Cyan't a bwa get no soup roun' here. (*To the door.*) I can't come to the door right now Mrs McCallum. I'm cooking, see. Cooking.

The knock comes to the door again, this time more insistent.

Ah what . . . (*Going towards the door.*) I said I can't come to the door right now, I'm . . .

As NIGEL *opens the door a little the person on the other side of the door kicks it open, knocking* NIGEL *down.*

(*As he is propelled backwards.*) Fucking hell. I'm cooking man. Can't you see I'm cooking?

PHIL *enters, looking around, his nose wrinkling with a slight contempt.* PHIL *is lean and fit and cocky, his wide-boy swagger screaming 'top-dog' at anyone who cares to listen. He wears an expensive suit beneath a long black raincoat and an open-necked shirt that suggests he might have had sex with someone he shouldn't have had in the last ten minutes and was in such a hurry to get out before her old man got back he forgot to put his tie back on. Or at least that's the look* PHIL*'s going for.* NIGEL *brushes himself off.*

Hey! You can't just do that man! You can't just come pushing in here, just knocking me over. Who are you?

PHIL. Who are you, more to the point?

NIGEL. I'm the bloke who lives here man. Who the fuck are you?

PHIL (*flashing a warrant card*). Anybody I want to be, sunshine.

NIGEL. Ah no, not again.

PHIL. Been visited before have we?

NIGEL. Yeah. No. Not for a while.

PHIL. You remember what it feels like though?

NIGEL. Yeah, I remember.

PHIL. Good, hold that feeling. Something tells me it's going to be a major part of your life from now on.

NIGEL. Ah what? You can't just come shoving in here acting like Mr Big Time. You gotta have a warrant or something. I got rights, you know.

PHIL. Yeah, right.

PHIL *makes himself at home.*

Nice place you've got here, Nigel. Like what you've done with it. What was it? *Changing Rooms Special* on Grunge?

NIGEL. What?

PHIL. It suits you.

NIGEL. Man, I don't know what's going on here, but I think there's been some sort of a mistake. I'm . . .

PHIL. You're Nigel Brunswick, 34 C Warrender Gardens. I mean that is your name, isn't it? Nigel?

NIGEL. Ah, no, no see . . . that's where you're wrong. My name is Salif, see. You got the wrong guy.

PHIL. Yeah. Wallet.

NIGEL. What?

PHIL. Give me your wallet.

NIGEL. What do you want my wallet for? You ain't gonna rob me.

PHIL (*grabbing* NIGEL*'s throat*). Give me your wallet you toe rag before I pop this head of yours like a big, fat pimple! You want that Nigel? You want your head to pop?

NIGEL. Aaagh! (*Tossing aside wallet.*) Take it! Take it! Man you rough.

PHIL *picks up the wallet and goes through the cards in it, reading the name on each before tossing it to the ground.*

PHIL. Nigel Brunswick. Nigel Brunswick. Nigel Brunswick. Nigel Brunswick.

NIGEL. It ain't official yet. I'm changing it soon though. I got the forms an' everyt'ing.

PHIL. Okay. So you're going to change your name. Not yet though, eh? I mean you're still going to be Nigel Brunswick for the immediate and foreseeable aren't you? For the purpose of this conversation I can still call you Nigel, can't I, Nigel?

NIGEL. Yeah. You can call me that.

PHIL. Good. Well Nigel, why don't you take a seat.

NIGEL. Why don't you take a seat, man? I mean, that's my job innit? I'm the host. You're in my house.

PHIL. It's housing association flat you cunt and don't you forget it. You don't own it. It doesn't belong to you. It belongs to the Housing Association. They're letting you stay here. All right?

NIGEL. Yeah . . . but I pay the . . .

PHIL. The fucking council pay the rent.

NIGEL. Yeah, okay, the council pay the rent, but it's my . . .

PHIL. You like living here Nigel?

NIGEL. What?

PHIL. 'Do you like living here?' It's a simple enough question.

NIGEL. Yeah. Yeah. I like it.

PHIL. Get on with your neighbours?

NIGEL. All right.

PHIL. I'd like living here if I was you. Better than some shit holes I've seen. It's nice. Nice stair. Clean.

NIGEL. That's Mrs Ma . . .

PHIL. Course all that could change. I mean, if you got arrested, things might be different. Your neighbours might start asking questions. You get arrested twice, definitely. When we come knocking down your door with a sledgehammer at four in the morning your neighbours are going to be on the blower faster than a bunch of Albanians who got their Euro-tunnel timetables mixed up. 'This is a nice block,' they'll say 'What you doing putting scum in a nice block like this. We've got kids here, we don't want coppers banging on the door night and day.' You get the picture, Nigel? This isn't your house. You're here on sufferance. Everything could change. Just like that. So why don't we sit down. Like I say. And get acquainted.

NIGEL. Man, this is so . . .

PHIL. This is so your life, Nigel. From here on in. I should've brought the book along, eh? The big red one. Tonight, Nigel Brunswick, this is *so* your life.

NIGEL sits. He sits like a naughty schoolboy with his hands clasped and his arms between his knees, waiting.

That's better now, isn't it?

Long pause. NIGEL gets jittery. He feels compelled to speak, but is scared to. Eventually it gets too much.

NIGEL. So what you want? You want something, right?

PHIL. I need a favour, Nigel.

NIGEL. What sort of favour?

PHIL. Wrong!

PHIL *kicks the coffee table over.*

NIGEL. Hey man, that's my . . .

PHIL. Nigel, will you concentrate. Never mind the table. Think about the immediate present and this situation you're in. The imbalance of power here. That's what you should be thinking about. The power I've got and the power you don't got. You got it yet?

NIGEL. Yeah.

PHIL. Okay. Now Nigel, I need a favour.

NIGEL. What can I do for you. Sir.

PHIL. Better.

PHIL *tosses a photograph to* NIGEL.

Recognise him?

NIGEL *(looking at picture)*. No.

PHIL. Look again.

NIGEL *(recognising picture)*. Are you serious?

PHIL. Deadly.

NIGEL. That's my brother man. Jesus, not a very good photo, is it?

PHIL. It's the best we could get off a fucking CCTV camera. If you've got a better one . . .

NIGEL. You know I ain't seen him since I was eighteen, right?

PHIL. I know that now, if that's what you're telling me.

NIGEL. Yeah sure. I ain't seen him in seven years man. Not since . . . What you want him for? I think you got your wires crossed somewhere. He's a good boy. I's the black sheep man.

PHIL. Nigel, you're the sugar plum fairy compared to this guy.

NIGEL. Hey man, I ain't no fairy. Who told you that? Just cause I ain't got a girlfriend . . . I ain't . . . aaaagh!

NIGEL *is flailing his hands in indignation.* PHIL *grabs a finger and twists his arm round his back. He forces his head down.*

PHIL. Okay, Nigel, somehow I don't think you're getting the seriousness of the situation. This man. This brother of yours.

I want him Nigel. I really want him. In the same way you want
Britney Spears to climb into your bed some night and whisper
'Nigel, you're the one, the only one for me you big sexy beast'
– that's how bad I want this guy. And you're the one who's
gonna get him for me, all wrapped up in a big pretty bow.

NIGEL. I ain't seen him man. How many times do I tell you.

PHIL. That's the past, Nigel. Let's talk about the future.

NIGEL. What future?

PHIL. You will see him.

NIGEL. I wo . . . Aagh! I will see him.

PHIL. You'll ask questions. You'll go looking . . . family, friends.
He's on the run, Nigel. He's desperate. He's running out of
places to hide. My guess is he'll end up here. And when he
does . . .

NIGEL. I won't let him in.

PHIL. You will let him in.

NIGEL. No sir, I swear I won't.

PHIL. You will. You will let him in.

NIGEL. I will let him in.

PHIL. And then what'll you do?

NIGEL. I won't speak to him.

PHIL. You will speak to him.

NIGEL. I will speak to him.

PHIL. You'll treat him like a long lost brother.

NIGEL. Which in many ways . . . aagh . . . yeah, okay . . . okay . . .

PHIL. Then what do you do?

NIGEL. Sir, I have no idea what then I will do. But I am open to
guidance, suggestions and advice.

PHIL. You'll call me.

NIGEL. I'll call you.

PHIL. You will call me.

NIGEL. Yes. I'll call you. I'll call you. I will call you.

PHIL. Good.

PHIL *gets up, regaining his composure.* NIGEL *attends to his hurting finger.*

NIGEL. Jesus man, what's he done?

PHIL *grabs* NIGEL *by the hair.*

PHIL. Christ, Nigel, don't you watch TV? Don't the words – 'We're the ones asking the questions' mean anything to you.

PHIL *throws* NIGEL *down. He stays on the floor, looking up.*

NIGEL. I'm just saying man. It must be something well fucked-up . . .

PHIL. You just concentrate on finding him. And clean this mess up. You live like a pig.

NIGEL *begins tidying.*

NIGEL. Man, you should be cleaning this. You the one caused it.

PHIL. Nigel. You don't want me cleaning up around here. You never know what I might find.

NIGEL *remembers the drugs. His eyes search the floor. Seeing it he goes to cover it.* PHIL *stands on his hand.*

Is this what you're looking for?

PHIL *takes the tin foil and sits, examining it.*

Well, well, well, what have we got here? This wouldn't be yours now, would it? Nigel? I said, this wouldn't be yours?

NIGEL. No.

PHIL. Funny that. It being in your house and everything.

NIGEL. It's not mine. Whatever it is. I mean, I don't know what it is . . .

PHIL. Good. You won't mind then, if I . . .

PHIL *finds something lying around to suck through, inspects it for cleanliness. He puts it in his mouth and takes out a lighter.*

NIGEL. Hey man, you can't do that . . .

PHIL. Why not? It's not yours.

NIGEL. No, but . . . nah, you can't do that. You're the police.

PHIL. Yeah, but it's not as if it's drugs now, is it? Because if it was drugs I'd have to arrest you.

NIGEL. It's not drugs, man. You can do what you want with it.

PHIL. Good.

*The policeman smokes up the drugs, keeping eye contact with
NIGEL at all times. It becomes apparent to NIGEL that he's in
a lot more shit than he thought he was in. He sits, his body
twisting and contracting, as if trying to make himself small and
unnoticeable until this big predator goes away. PHIL exhales,
lies back.*

Man, you wouldn't believe the day I've had.

NIGEL. Me neither, man. Me neither.

*In the lights down/change of scene, we see PHIL leaving,
smiling and satisfied, while MRS MAC keeps close watch from
her door.*

2.

*Lights come up on MARCO, sitting in the stairs outside his flat,
engrossed in his Gameboy. MARCO is in his mid-teens, small in
stature, of mixed race, predominantly Afro-Caribbean. MARCO
tries to concentrate on the game he is playing – the sound effects
of which are heard – but it is difficult for him to concentrate for
the sounds coming through the wall of a couple noisily having sex.
MARCO's player crashes and burns.*

MARCO. Oh for fuck sake mum, knock it on the head!

*The noise abates. A voice is heard going 'Ssshhh!' followed by
muffled breathless laughter. MARCO turns back for a new
game but soon the noise starts up again. NIGEL rushes out of
his flat and bundles up the stairs.*

NIGEL. Marco? Marco?

*NIGEL comes rushing up, just as MARCO's mum reaches
a crescendo. He is about to let rip with his ultra-exciting news
but is distracted and does a double take.*

Jesus, Marco . . . you'll never believe . . . (*Double take.*) Is that
your mum?

MARCO. Nah, Jennifer Lopez just popped in for a wank.

*NIGEL stops and giggles a bit at how cool it would be if it
were really true. MARCO's mum finally finishes. MARCO
crashes and burns.*

NIGEL (*looking at Gameboy score*). Jesus man, that's shit.

MARCO. You do better with your mum grunting and groaning next door.

NIGEL. Aw man, I thought she'd knocked it on the head? Got herself a proper job?

MARCO. She's not cut out for a career in retail. Apparently. That's what that cunt from Kwik-Save told her. Something to do with threatening to shove a cucumber up some old dear's arse. I forget the details. (NIGEL *smiles and nods*.) What you doing here anyway? I thought you was having some 'me' time.

NIGEL. Ah, fuck, fuck, fuck – that's what I came to tell you man. I got the heat on me, man. I got the heat on me big style.

MARCO. Wha' you mean, you got the heat on you? What you been doing?

NIGEL. Nothing man, I swear. Babylon using me. Babylon using me for a stoolie. Me own brother man. They want me to set up me own brother.

MARCO. You ain't got no brother.

NIGEL. Sure I have. Half brother.

MARCO. What half brother?

NIGEL. Man, you shoulda been there. Big cunt, just kicks down the fucking door. Kicks down me door see. And I'm like – hey man, what you doing coming in here kicking down people's door man. That ain't right. An he gets me right, and he's twisting my arm right, and he's like – Nigel Brunswick you are in so much shit cos I is the law and the law is down on your arse big time.

MARCO. Bullshit.

NIGEL. No bullshit. This guy's like Rambo and Shaft and that cunt off 'The Bill' – the crooked one. This guy's laying into me. He's like – Nigel, I am your worst nightmare bwa, I am the sound and the fury, I am God's wing-ed Chariot come down to smoke your arse. You do what I tell you or you fucking cop it, and I'm like – no way copper, you never turn me into your stooge, and then he picks up me brown and he . . .

MARCO. He what?

NIGEL. He picks up me brown.

MARCO. Ah fuck sake Nigel. You promised me . . .

NIGEL. Yeah. Yeah. An you promised me you'd stop calling me Nigel and start calling me Salif but I don't see that happening nowhere, bwa. An beside. It just one night. One night out of three hundred an sixty-five I decide to get me some brown stuff an have me some 'me' time. Bwa got a right. Tough world out there, bwa. You need the edges smooth.

MARCO. So he busted you?

NIGEL *spots a half-smoked joint in* MARCO*'s ashtray. He picks it up and looks it over, fussing with it. At some point, when he considers it smokeable, he will light it up.*

NIGEL. Busted me? Ain't you been listening. This ain't normal cop, this is super cop. He don't bust me. He pick up me brown an say – this yours? – and I say – no – an he say, you don't mind if I, then . . . – an' cunt goes an' spark up me brown, right in front of me, an he's fucking smoking it see. In front of me. That ain't no normal cop.

MARCO. You're tripping, Nigel.

NIGEL. I ain't fucking tripping man. This guy want me an this guy got me an I'm crapping it man. I'm fucking crapping it.

MARCO. Okay man, okay. Jus' tell me about it. Real slow. Who's this guy they want? Who's this brother?

NIGEL. My brother see. My half brother. Karim. My father, right – the guy who fuck me mother to get me – he got this family, see. Way over on the other side. Respec'able see. Me mum, she jus' some slap an' typical for him see, she jus' some ride. He wasn't expecting no me, see. He wasn't expecting me. He one of these guys just had his cake an' then he didn't want to eat it. Three times I seen that cunt, man. Three times I seen that cunt, man, three times, and two of them was when I was nicking shit out of his shops. I tell you, I'm like Leonardo di Caprio in that movie man. They put a mask on me an' throw me in a dungeon an' that other cunt get all my respec'. Karim, his other son, that the one Babylon want. Won't even tell me what he done. I told him – Robocop – that bwa he never did no wrong, man. Never. Him the good boy. Him a fucking Moslem for fuck sake, a holy roller. That boy sneeze without a hanky he got to crawl to fucking Mecca just to get right with it. I tell him I'm the bad boy. I'm the black sheep. Cops come looking for anybody should be me. I fucking crack off a few caps in their honky arses, bwa. Gangster, see. Respec' me.

MARCO. Jesus Nigel.

NIGEL. What?

MARCO. There's a picture emerging here and I don't fucking like it one bit.

NIGEL. What?

MARCO. He's a fucking Moslem man!

NIGEL. Yeah, I told you that. Moslem. Good boy.

MARCO. Jesus Nigel. They got a fucking hard-on for Moslems nowadays man. Moslems are the new gangsters. Moslems are like the worst shit ever.

NIGEL. Ah. Nah. Nah, nah, nah see. He ain't no Malcolm X Moslem see. He just a Paki Moslem. It's not the same thing. He ain't a cool Moslem see. He jus' a good little boy go to Mosque every Sunday.

MARCO. Fucking Hell, Nigel. Where you been? It's the fucking Paki Moslems that's been at it.

NIGEL. At what?

MARCO. At fucking everything man. Bombing people, gassing people, driving fucking aeroplanes into the fucking Empire State Building! Man, if your brother . . . If your brother's one of them. Fuck. You're fucked, Nigel. If they're after him they ain't letting go til they caught him. That means you. They ain't letting go you.

NIGEL. What? Ah shit. You sure.

MARCO. Ain't you watch the news, bwa?

NIGEL. Hey – don't need no weather man to see which way the wind blow.

MARCO. You fucking do. That's exac'ly what you need. You need Michael Fish an' Ian MacKaskill an' fucking John Kettley an' that skinny bird too. It's fucking raining man. You need to know when it's raining or you gonna go out with no fucking umbrella an get soaked man.

NIGEL. Marco? What the fuck are you talking about man?

MARCO. I'm talking about you man. I'm talking about how screwed you really are.

NIGEL. So what's me s'posed to do?

MARCO. Do what they say man. This is fucking serious. They'll take you out to that island and torture your fucking arse.

NIGEL. What? What island?

MARCO. They fucking will. Gloves off man. They can do what
they want soon as them fucking Pakis are involved.

NIGEL. But I don't know nothing,

MARCO. You better make something up then. And fast. This ain't
no game Nigel. Those cunts is serious.

NIGEL. Hey. Him want serious him get serious.

MARCO. Nigel, ain't no joke man. Ain't no joke. Whole world's
changing. This ain't like before when your social worker go
breezing in tell them 'Go easy on Nigel, he just a fuck up'.
Ain't nothing your social worker gonna do when the fucking
C.I.A come knocking.

NIGEL. C.I.A? What that? Like 'Mission Impossible'?

MARCO. Jesus Nigel, you are so fucked, man.

NIGEL. Yeah. I thought that was the case.

*MARCO's mum is heard giggling in the next room. The sex
starts up again.*

MARCO. Ah fuck, let's get out of here. I can't think with all that
going on.

*NIGEL sticks around for a bit to listen to MARCO's mum
having sex.*

Nigel. Come on.

NIGEL. Yeah, I's coming.

*NIGEL smiles, giggles, unconsciously puts a hand to his
crotch.*

MARCO. Nige!

NIGEL. Yeah. Coming.

NIGEL exits.

3.

Later that night. MRS McCALLUM *is sitting in her armchair watching TV, a news broadcast, the words of which we can hear.*

NEWSREADER. Home news now, and three men arrested last night in separate raids in North London and Glasgow were today remanded in custody at the High Court in Glasgow charged with offences under the Prevention of Terrorism Act. The men, thought to be of North African origin were taken to a secure police station in the Govan area of the city for further questioning. London, and Heathrow airport was again the subject of increased sec . . .

MRS MAC switches off the TV. She turns to her husband, Harry, or rather his photograph, which is all she has left.

MRS MAC. I don't know, Harry, Hell in a hand basket, that's where we're heading. I've a good mind to write to 'Points of View'. What do you mean what am I talking about? This! Taking off 'Nash Bridges' and putting on the news! 'News'? It's been the same story for the last two years. You tell me what's new about that?

She gets to her feet to put away her cup.

I thought you liked 'Nash Bridges'. Oh, he is not a poof, Harry! He was married to that slut, what was her name? The drunk who went off with that Spaniard.

Meanwhile NIGEL is leaving MARCO's, muttering to himself.

NIGEL. Oh man, C.I.A? What the fuck do I know about the fucking C.I.A?

He drops his keys.

NIGEL. Ah shit!

MRS MAC hears the keys falling. Her whole body goes on alert. She seems to sniff the air.

MRS MAC. Who's that now? At this time? I will not leave it alone.

NIGEL (*still muttering*). Can't do anything right. Nigel. Nigel. Can't even open your own fucking door.

NIGEL gets down on his hands and knees to find his keys. MRS MAC opens her door to see what's going on.

MRS MAC. Who's there? Nigel? Is that you?

NIGEL. Yeah, it's me, Mrs McCallum. I dropped my keys, see. I's looking for them. Okay. I's looking for them.

MRS MAC. Really Nigel, it's gone eleven.

NIGEL (*to himself*). I know what fucking time it is.

MRS MAC. People are trying to sleep.

NIGEL (*shouted up*). Look Mrs McCallum I've got me a few problems right now. I ain't really in the mood for no 'keep the noise down' lectures tonight, all right?

MRS MAC. I know what's going on, Nigel.

NIGEL. Nothing's going on Mrs McCallum. I just lost my keys, see.

MRS MAC. Oh really Nigel, there's no need to be so coy. I know all about your 'problems'. How thick do you think these walls are? I heard you. You and your 'friend'. All that shouting and banging. Do you think we're all deaf or something. And really, I've just got to say, Nigel – no matter how much trouble you think you're in, it's really no excuse for rudeness, now, is it?

NIGEL. No, you're right, Mrs McCallum. It's no excuse for rudeness. No excuse at all. I'm very sorry. Please accept my apology, all right?

MRS MAC. Oh Nigel, you wouldn't be the first young man to get himself into trouble. But really, you shouldn't go to those people, not even as a last resort. They're leeches, Nigel. Parasites. Preying on the weak and the vulnerable. Of course *I* knew him. As soon as I clapped eyes on him I knew him. I said to myself – 'I know you, mister. I've seen your type before'. 'Bloodsuckers of the poor' my husband used to call them. He had very strong views on usury, Mr McCallum, very strong. If he was still around that young man would've left here with more than a flea buzzing in his ear, I can tell you.

NIGEL. Hey, slow down Mrs McCallum. You're losing me now. What's that usury? What's that got to do with me?

MRS MAC. Usury, Nigel. The lending of money for profit or gain. Say somebody gives you ten pounds today on condition you to pay them back fifteen tomorrow, and boy, you'd better pay, that's usury, Nigel.

NIGEL. Ain't that what banks do?

MRS MAC. They're all the same thing Nigel. They might dress themselves up in suits and ties but they're all the same thing. Usurers and Shylocks. And they should be shot. Every last one of them. Or so my husband used to say.

NIGEL. He sounds like a very wise man, Mrs McCallum. Mr McCallum that is. Very wise and just a little bit deranged.

MRS MAC. Oh he was, Nigel. A very wise man. 'Never a borrower or a lender be'. That was his motto. You can see for yourself the wisdom in that. Just look at the misery it's causing you.

NIGEL. Me? Oh, nah. Nah, nah, nah Mrs McCallum. You got it all wrong, see. I ain't in debt.

MRS MAC. No, Nigel. Of course not. Don't worry, dear, your secret's safe with me.

MRS MAC *turns to go back inside as* NIGEL *tries to protest.*

NIGEL. No really, I's . . .

MRS MAC (*turning back*). The important thing is to learn from the experience. And hide your benefit books. They take them for collateral I hear.

MRS MAC *goes back inside, smiling sympathetically.* NIGEL *leans against the wall, then slides into a sitting position, a desperate smile fixed on his face.*

NIGEL. Oh, I's fucked. Fucked, fucked, fucked.

4.

A deserted play park. NIGEL *is sitting on the swings waiting for* PHIL. *He looks disconsolate and finds it hard to settle. He goes in his pocket for his walkman earpieces and puts them in, hoping the music will distract him from his plight. He tries to hum along but is not really in the mood. The tune is not recognisable until he sings the chorus. It is 'Dy-na-mi-tee' by Ms Dynamite.* NIGEL *becomes aware of a change in the environment, a feeling, just a feeling, that he is being watched. He takes the earpieces out and looks around. Nothing. He puts the earpieces back in and continues humming along but the tune becomes slower as his eyes move left to right, searching to see if anybody is coming.*

His instincts are right but his direction is wrong. MARCO *is sneaking up behind him.*

MARCO. Boo!

NIGEL. Aaaaagh!

NIGEL, *being wound up already, jumps a metaphorical six feet in the air.* MARCO *laughs.*

Jesus Marco, I could've had a heart attack.

MARCO. Don't talk shit.

NIGEL. Hey, people have heart attacks. Especially people who are as wound up as me.

MARCO. Serves you right for blocking up your ears. Ain't you heard man, it's a jungle out there. Don't see no antelope loping around with their Walkmans on full blast. You need to be alert man. Ready to run at the slightest change in temperature. Pow! Off! I tell you, any antelope grooving to the new Darius tune, that new Darius tune is gonna be the second last thing that antelope is ever going to hear.

NIGEL. Ain't fucking Darius.

MARCO. Bet it fucking is.

NIGEL. It ain't.

MARCO. Bet it is.

NIGEL. Fucking hell Marco, how many times do I have to tell you. I only voted for him as a joke.

MARCO. You walked half a mile to find a phone that worked.

NIGEL. Yeah. It was a joke, see. Anyway. What's the last thing?

MARCO. What last thing?

NIGEL. The last thing the antelope hear man?

MARCO. Oh. You mean tiger slurp?

NIGEL. Tiger slurp?

MARCO. Yeah. Tiger slurp. The sound a tiger makes when he's slurping on some juicy antelope dick.

MARCO *demonstrates the Tiger slurp.*

NIGEL. Man, you know fuck all about antelopes. I bet they don't even have dicks. And even if they had, bet the fucking tiger doesn't eat it. Tigers are well hard man. They ain't into none of that nancy shit.

MARCO. Yeah, but round here it ain't the tigers you got to worry about, is it?

NIGEL. You don't know about none of that neither, so fuck off.

MARCO can see that NIGEL is upset about something. He gives him a little time and space before speaking.

MARCO. So what you doing up here anyway? Bit old for the swings ain't ya?

NIGEL. Waiting for super-cop ain't I? He told me to meet him here.

MARCO. Fucking drama queen. Why can't he just go round your house like a normal person?

NIGEL. Well he ain't no normal person. Is he?

MARCO. Yeah, I forgot. He's . . . super-cop!

NIGEL. It ain't funny Marco. I'm bricking it.

MARCO. He ain't as bad as you say he is. Can't be.

NIGEL. Look at me, Marco. You think if this guy wasn't everything I say he is I'd be as wound up as this? Do you? You think I'd be chasing all over like a blue-arsed fly if this was normal cop?

NIGEL is on the verge of tears. MARCO sees he is serious.

MARCO. You ain't heard anything then? About that brother of yours? He ain't turned up 'as 'e?

NIGEL. He ain't turning up here, is he? Ain't seen him in seven years, ain't just going to turn up now, no matter what Babylon think. I've been everywhere, everywhere, man. Nobody seen him. Nobody even heard his name for years.

MARCO. So what you going to say to him? Super-cop?

NIGEL. Ain't a lot I can say, is there? Sorry Mr Policeman, but as of yet I have not been contacted by any international terrorist organisation nor have I been able to ascertain the whereabouts of my estranged half-brother who may or may not be a member of the aforementioned terrorist organisation. It's a fucking joke, innit? I'll tell you another thing. I don't think it's fucking legal. If they wants me to join the police force they should give me a fucking hat at least. Then I'd know they wasn't just taking the piss.

MARCO. I don't think they're taking the piss, Nigel.

NIGEL. No, neither do I. This ain't a good situation, is it Marco? I mean, dope-smoking psycho cops with a licence to kill ain't ever good news, is it?

MARCO. Maybe you should take off for a bit. Ever think about that? Just leg it.

NIGEL. Where would I go? This is my home, man. I don't know anywhere else. I can't just take off. I only got that flat cause I's mental. I ain't giving it up now.

MARCO. You ain't mental, Nigel.

NIGEL. Yeah I am.

MARCO. What about your mum? Won't she put a roof over you for a bit?

NIGEL. Me Mum? Me mum don't want me.

MARCO. She's your mum, Nige. Course she wants you.

NIGEL. Nah. She got herself set up with some white guy now. Fucking plumber or something. She don't want me. She don't want me anywhere near.

MARCO. Don't she love you?

NIGEL. Course she loves me. She just don't want me around, okay. Too much of a reminder, ain't I? Too much of an embarrassment.

MARCO. Cause you're black?

NIGEL. Nah, cause I's . . . Don't matter why! She don't want me. Full stop. She's got her reasons.

NIGEL *sits for a while, reliving memories that are obviously less than pleasant. But soon he smiles.*

I went round there last week. Did I tell ya? Thought she might have that cunt's number. I got me a sister, can you believe that? A lickle sister, man. Sweet.

MARCO. Didn't she tell you?

NIGEL. How can she tell me, man? I ain't got no phone.

MARCO. No. Course.

NIGEL. A lickle sister man. Sweet.

MARCO. So what's she called?

NIGEL. My sister?

MARCO. Yeah.

NIGEL. They's . . . They's called her Sarah, but I's called
her . . . Miss Dynamitee-ee.

They smile, bashful.

A lickle sister man. Sweet.

MARCO. Did she have his number then? Your dad's?

NIGEL. Nah. She didn't have nothing man. Said he was probably
dead. I said – nah, if he was dead they woulda told me. She
says – well, she don't say fucking nothing really. Just laughs.
The way them teachers used to laugh when you answered a
question wrong. Fuck it. I ain't running. This is my home, man.
Why should I run? What I do? Eh? Eh? I's the innocent in this.

MARCO. They woulda told you, Nigel. If he was dead. They
gotta.

NIGEL. Do I look as if I care? Do I? That man a stranger to me.
Stranger to me live, stranger to me dead. I ain't taking the rap
cause that tart can't keep her fucking legs crossed, man. I ain't
suffering for it! Shit. What time is it? (*Looks at watch.*) He
shoulda been here by now. (*Getting up.*) Fuck it, I's leaving.
I ain't at his beck and call. I ain't his bitch he can keep me
waiting like this. (*Shouting.*) You hear that copper? You hear it?
I! Ain't! Your! Bitch!

NIGEL *looks around the deserted area. His courage goes. He
sheepishly sits down.*

Fuck it. I give him five more minutes man. Five minutes, that's
all.

Pause.

MARCO. Sometimes I think my mum don't love me.

NIGEL. What?

MARCO. Nothing. I was just saying . . . Sometimes I think my
mum don't love me.

Pause. NIGEL *smiles mischievously.*

NIGEL. Give her a fiver, man. She'll love you then.

MARCO. Oh fuck! You're sick man.

NIGEL. Yeah. But you know it true. Come on. Let's get the fuck
out of here. Get a bottle of wine an go sit in the park. Come
on, I'll get you some bread. You can feed them fucking ducks
you like.

MARCO. What about Super-cop?

NIGEL. Fuck Super-cop. If he want me he can come and find me. He know where I live.

> MARCO *hesitates.* NIGEL *smiles and cocks his head in the direction of the park.* MARCO *smiles and joins him.*

5.

PHIL *is banging on* NIGEL's *door.* MRS MAC *is cleaning the stairs.*

PHIL. Nigel! Nigel! Open up! It's me, Phil! Nigel!

MRS MAC. There's no use banging like that, you know. He's not in.

PHIL. Oh yeah? And what would you know?

MRS MAC. Well, for one thing, if he was in he'd answer the door.

PHIL. No shit, Sherlock.

MRS MAC. And for another, I just saw him going along the High Street.

PHIL. Shit.

> PHIL *turns to hurry after* NIGEL. MRS MAC *calls after him.*

MRS MAC. He was getting on a bus. If you run you might just catch him. They're not the fastest buses in the world.

> PHIL *is stopped in his tracks.*

Oh dear, how sad, never mind.

PHIL. Hey wait . . . You live here don't you?

MRS MAC. I most certainly do. Not that it's any of your beeswax.

PHIL. You know the guy who lives here? Nigel? Any idea where he was going?

MRS MAC. I think you'll find we keep ourselves to ourselves around here, young man.

PHIL. Yeah, but you know him though? Nigel?

MRS MAC. Of course I know Nigel. This isn't one of those stairs where nobody knows who the people living next door to them

are, if that's what you were thinking. We know our neighbours.
Imagine living in a block like this and not knowing who was
on the other side of the wall? Anything could be going on. Of
course they say that's 'the norm' now, whatever that's supposed
to mean. In my day we knew our neighbours. We'd look out for
each other. Our neighbours were our friends. Nowadays you
dare so much as nod your head in another person's direction
they look at you as if you're mad. Everybody's so scared
nowadays, and what have they got to be scared of? A little
conversation? A polite nod of the head? It's hardly the
Luftwaffe, now, is it?

PHIL. I don't know love, it's a scary world out there.

MRS MAC. Scary world? Hmph. You're just like all those old
biddies down my lunch club. 'Oh I never go out anymore, it's
too dangerous, I'm too scared'. Of course you're scared, I tell
them, you never go out. If you went out once in a while you
wouldn't be so scared. I tell them till I'm blue in the face, but
will they listen? No, they go home, bolt the door, sit there
shaking, waiting for some maniac who never turns up. They
might as well be in prison. And these are people who fought in
wars, you know? Or if they didn't fight they certainly listened
to the bombs falling night after night. Now that was a scary
world. You couldn't sort Hitler out with a clip around the lug.

PHIL. No, I suppose not.

MRS MAC. And it's no use you smiling that stupid smile at me,
young man. I know exactly who you are. You may scare Nigel
with that hard man act but I think you'll find I'm a far tougher
proposition. Moneylenders? At least the pawnbrokers had the
sense to ask for security, even if it was only your winter coat.
They never had to resort to kicking down people's doors.

PHIL. What? Oh no . . . You've got it all wrong love. I'm a police
officer, look . . .

PHIL *shows her his warrant card.*

MRS MAC. Oh, anyone could make one of those. I'm sure my
grandson has one just as good.

PHIL. No, seriously, I am a policeman. Look, can I talk to you.
It's important.

MRS MAC. What do you mean? Important?

PHIL. It is! Look, just let me come in for a few minutes, will you?
I'll explain it all over a nice cup of tea.

MRS MAC goes inside. PHIL *follows her. He pauses before he goes in, smiling.*

6.

Later that night. MRS MAC *is in her flat. She looks worried. We see* NIGEL *returning home. He has the remnants of his wine with him. He is relaxed and happy, again singing 'Dynamite-e' He bumps into the walls a bit. The noise spooks* MRS MAC. *She opens her door a crack and looks out.*

NIGEL. Good night Mrs McCallum.

> MRS MAC *jumps back inside and closes the door, terrified.* NIGEL *looks baffled.*

7.

Next morning. NIGEL'*s flat.* PHIL *is inside, quietly nosing around. He is talking on his mobile phone, quietly but audibly, as if someone was sleeping in the next room. As he talks he goes to the kitchen and switches on the kettle.*

PHIL. No, all I'm saying is – why waste Special Branch's money on it? We don't need that level of surveillance around here- local knowledge, that's where it's at. Yeah, course I do. There's a guy I'm working on right now in fact- cunt's so scared he'll phone it in. Yeah, soon as it happens. Trust me, Joe – you keep the Super off my back a few more days and we'll all come out of this smelling of roses. Forget Special Branch! We'll be living in an Islamic Republic before Special Branch get up off their arses to see what all the noise is about. I know these people, Joe. I know how they work. I'm inside their heads. I'm like the fucking Jesuits, you know – give me a scrote for . . . The Jesuits. (*Pause.*) The Jesuits. (*Pause.*) No, they're a . . . Oh fuck off you thick cunt!

> PHIL *turns off his phone, his face displaying the displeasure he feels at being surrounded all his life by idiots.*

> *He takes a seat, lights a cigarette.* NIGEL *comes out in his boxer shorts, half asleep, rubbing his eyes and his genitals and*

anything else that needs rubbing. He doesn't see PHIL *at first, and heads for the kitchen.*

PHIL. Kettle's on.

NIGEL *turns and points at* PHIL. *A strange hyperventilating noise comes out of his mouth. Eventually he manages to speak.*

NIGEL. What the fuck are you doing in my house?

PHIL. Hey, that's no way to greet an old friend.

NIGEL. I'm not your friend you cunt! How the fuck did you get into my house? I . . . I . . . (NIGEL *is finding it difficult to speak.*) You broke into my flat, you cunt!

PHIL. Well maybe I wouldn't have to break into your flat if you started actually bothering to do what you say you're going to do. You know? Do what you say. Just once in your stupid life.

NIGEL. What you talking about, man?

PHIL. Yesterday! If I say meet me somewhere you fucking meet me there. Do you understand? I do not take kindly to being dicked with!

NIGEL. What you talking about? I was there man, where the fuck was you?

PHIL. Where do you think I was?

NIGEL. I don't know where you was man, but you wasn't at the swings when you said you'd be. I waited there.

PHIL. I was there.

NIGEL. When man? When was you there? Maybe you want to check your fucking clock, cause I was there at four and I was there at four thirty and you wasn't there. What's up? You got some cheap Japanese watch or something?

The advancing PHIL *shoves his watch into* NIGEL*'s face.*

PHIL. Does this look like a cheap watch to you, Nigel? Does it?

NIGEL (*inspecting watch*). What's that man? A Carter?

PHIL. It's pronounced Cartier you toe rag.

NIGEL. Nah man. Cartier got an I in it. Just between the t and the e. That' a Carter watch you got there man. Somebody's been at it with you. You buy that off Del Boy or something.

PHIL (*grabbing* NIGEL*'s throat*). Christ Nigel, if you knew the sort of pressure I'm under you would can it with the Ben Elton routine. I'm not in the mood, okay?

NIGEL. Okay. Okay. No need for violence. I's co-operating with you ain't I?

PHIL. I don't know Nigel, are you?

NIGEL. Yeah, I'm co-operating. I'm doing everything you said, man. What's wrong with you? Why you got to be so rough all the time. Ain't my fault you got a dodgy watch.

PHIL. This watch is not dodgy.

NIGEL. Look at the clock, man. You at least an hour fast, man. At least an hour.

PHIL. What? Oh Christ Nigel, I don't believe this. You forgot to put your clocks forward. Didn't you?

NIGEL. What?

PHIL. The clocks. They went forward at the weekend, you dick.

NIGEL. What they do that for?

PHIL. They do it every year.

NIGEL. Well nobody told me. And that's the sort of shit people should tell me. You know? (*Going to mirror.*) Aw fuck man, look what you did to my neck. You a bully, you know that?

PHIL. I'm a . . . Christ Nigel, you'd better start spilling your guts in the next thirty seconds or you're going to find out what a bully really is.

NIGEL. I know what a bully is! (PHIL *moves towards him.*) Okay, okay, I'm talking. What you want to talk about?

PHIL. Fucking Karim you dozy bastard. Any other reason you can think of why I'd be round here wasting my time on shit like you? Or do you really think it's your sparkling conversation that keeps dragging me back for more?

NIGEL. Hey, I was considered a great beauty in me youth. Maybe I's still got some of that going on for me. Must be some reason you get so agitated around me all the time.

PHIL *punches* NIGEL.

NIGEL. Aaagh! What the fuck you do that for?

PHIL. Did you see the news this morning Nigel? Did you? There's fucking tanks at Heathrow airport. The whole country's shitting itself. You should think really carefully about that, Nigel. Because me giving you a slap doesn't mean so very much when the whole country's shitting itself. Does it now? In fact

I'd go as far as to say you could film me shoving a red hot
poker up your skinny half-breed arse and show it on the six o
clock news and all Mr and Mrs Joe Public are going to say is
'Thank fuck somebody's doing something'. This is not the time
to have a brown skin and a wise-arse disposition, Nigel. Do
you understand that? That sort of shit can get you killed!

PHIL *has been man-handling* NIGEL *during this exchange.*
NIGEL *snaps. He starts pushing back.*

NIGEL. Yeah? Go on then! Kill me!

PHIL. What?

NIGEL. You heard me! Kill me! Do me fucking in! Do you think
I give a fuck! Do you think it's going to make my life any
worse, you bastard! Go on! Kill me! Fucking kill me! I don't
give a fuck! You hear me?

PHIL *backs off.*

PHIL. Look Nigel . . .

NIGEL. Don't 'Look Nigel' me! Kill me! If you're going to kill
me just fucking kill me cause I don't give a fuck anymore! I's
doing everything you fucking say, man, everything you fucking
say, and all I's getting is you coming in here shouting 'Where
the fuck was you yesterday' when where the fuck I was
yesterday was where the fuck you fucking told me to be
yesterday you fuck! Kill me! Go on! Kill me! I don't care
anymore!

PHIL. Jesus Nigel, calm down for fuck sake. None of us wants
this.

NIGEL. No? I thought that's what you did want? I've got a brown
skin and a wise arse dispo-whatever-the-fuck-it-was, so kill
me! I don't care. What's wrong with you, man? Ain't you read
my file? I do not! React! Well! To Pressure!

NIGEL *sticks his thumb in his mouth, stands on one leg, wraps
his free hand around his head and hums repetitively – a
strange rhythmic droning noise that totally freaks out* PHIL.

PHIL. Jesus Nigel, okay. Look. Stop. I'm sorry for fuck sake.
Calm down. I'm sorry, eh? I got it wrong. Okay Nigel? I got it
wrong. Jesus. Stop that fucking humming will you. You sound
like a fucking giraffe. I'm not here to piss you off, Nigel. I just
need your help, okay? We're at fucking war here. We're
fighting a bunch of fucking ghosts. We don't know who they
are or where they are or what they're planning. All we know

for sure is they're out there somewhere and as long as they're out there we're in a lot of fucking danger! Do you understand Nigel? Do you? This is serious!

NIGEL (*stopping abruptly*). Well pissing me off is not going to help.

PHIL. No.

NIGEL. You know, if I was looking for somebody's help I would not go round their house shouting at them.

PHIL. It's just the way we work, Nigel. My boss does it to me all the time. He shouts at me, I shout at you. It's a management technique for fuck sake.

NIGEL. Well it ain't fucking working is it?

PHIL. No, it's not. Look Nigel, maybe I've handled this wrong, but you've got to believe me. I wouldn't be here unless it was really important.

NIGEL. Important for who?

PHIL. For everybody. Look Nigel, I know you're doing your best to help us. And we're grateful for it, really we are.

NIGEL. Yeah?

PHIL. Yeah. Course we are.

NIGEL. Well I ain't seeing no fucking gratitude, man. All I's seeing is fucking brutality and burglary. I can't believe you just come in my house.

PHIL. We are grateful, Nigel. Look, I got you something.

   PHIL *takes out two jiffy bags filled with powder.*

NIGEL. What's that, man? Drugs?

PHIL. Yeah. I couldn't remember what you liked, so I got a bit of both.

NIGEL. Drugs? Man, you shouldn't be giving me drugs.

PHIL. Why not?

NIGEL. They make me unstable.

PHIL. Who says?

NIGEL. Doctors. Doctors say.

PHIL. What do doctors know? Go on. Take them. I'll make some tea, eh? We'll chill for a bit.

NIGEL. This is a trap, ain't it?

PHIL. God Nigel, you are so suspicious. If you don't want them you don't have to take them. I'll make some tea anyway. We can have a chat, eh? Nice and civilised.

NIGEL *is left with the drugs. He eyes them tentatively. Every fibre of his being wants to grab them, but he is scared.* PHIL *returns with two steaming mugs and sits. He smiles up at* NIGEL *as he removes the tobacco from the top of a cigarette. He takes some heroin from the bag with the handle of a teaspoon and puts it in the cigarette.* NIGEL *watches fascinated.*

PHIL. I saw this on 'The Sopranos'.

NIGEL. Man, you a funny copper, you know that? I thought you was supposed to be getting this shit off the streets.

PHIL *puts the removed tobacco back in the cigarette, lights it, then hands the cigarette to* NIGEL.

PHIL. Yeah, well, desperate times call for desperate measures. Besides, when it comes to drugs we've pretty much given up. If you ask me some Afghani Warlord's called in a favour, cause these last few months we've been swimming in this shit. (PHIL *watches as* NIGEL *smokes.*) So we friends again?

NIGEL. Hey, you know I can't stay mad at you for long.

PHIL. Good. Come and sit then. Come on, I've made you some tea.

NIGEL *sits, still not entirely convinced that 'Nice Phil's' evil twin has entirely left the building. But the heroin is starting to calm him.*

So, what you been up to lately, Nigel? Anything good.

NIGEL. Been trying to track down me half brother for this mad copper I know.

PHIL. Yeah? So how's that working out?

NIGEL. It ain't.

PHIL. You sure about that, Nige? You wouldn't be holding out on me, would you?

NIGEL. Hey, if I knew something I tell you, man. But I don't. He gone, man. Long gone. Ain't nobody seen hide or hair. (*Seeing* PHIL*'s disappointment.*) Man, you got a real Wile. E. Coyote thing going on there, ain't you?

PHIL. Yeah well, it's important, Nigel.

NIGEL. I know it is. I know it is. But sometimes you just got to
realise that the reality of a situation ain't exactly as you
perceive it. You ask a hundred people if they see a roadrunner
round here and they all say no – sometimes you just gotta
accept that nobody's seen that roadrunner, man. He just ain't
been here.

PHIL. He's your brother, though, isn't he? He isn't a roadrunner.
He's your brother.

NIGEL. Yeah, he's my brother, but we ain't close. Ain't like we
grew up together or nothing. Ain't like I's going round his
house every Christmas singing 'Silent Night'. Shit, I didn't
even know the cunt existed til I was fourteen. I'm coming out
of school one day, right, and I see this little Paki kid waiting
there. He's looking at me, see, but I don't think nothing of it.
People often look at me, you know? I got striking features or
something. Anyway, after that, everywhere I go I see him, man.
This Paki kid. He's like my fucking shadow man. My little
Paki shadow. I walk, he walk. I stop, he stop. Eventually I just
stop and fucking stare at him see, like this, see – (NIGEL
shows PHIL *his best stern stare.*) – and I'm like 'Okay Shorty,
spill'. He's got this little posh voice man, and he's like – 'I know
you, you're Nigel aren't you?' And I'm like – 'Hey, I know
who the fuck I am. Who the fuck are you?' And he goes –
'My name is Karim. I think we might be related'. And I go –
'Yeah?' An he go – 'Yeah. I think you're my brother, Nigel'.
And I'm like – 'Go away, kid, I don't have no brother' , but he
just stands there right, this sweet little kid, and he go – and
listen to this – he go 'Neither do I, but I think you might be
him'. (NIGEL *raises an eyebrow to suggest this is the wisest,
most profound sentence he has ever heard in his life.*) Neither
do I, but I think you might be him. (*He waits for* PHIL *to see
the wonder of this, but* PHIL *hasn't been smoking smack.*) He
heard his uncles talking see. Laughing at his old man. Keep
going on about 'Papa's little white boy'. That what they call
him. Papa. Like he the big daddy or something – baby-mothers
all over the shop. Like he some kind of Mac. (NIGEL *makes
contemptuous sound with his saliva.*)

PHIL. He tracked you down? How old was he then?

NIGEL. I donno. Twelve?

PHIL. Twelve, Jesus. Resourceful.

NIGEL. Yeah. He resourceful. He a smart kid. Anyway – I'm like
fuck off kid, I ain't your brother. I ain't no Paki, am I? But then
I tell my mother. And I know from her face, man. I know from
her silence. I know from her little tart eyes man. That kid
telling the truth. It's like when I was little and I'd be going to
school an people would be shouting– Paki, hey Paki – Paki,
Paki, Paki, and I'm looking but I don't see no Paki. And they're
shouting at me see, and I'm like – I'm fucking English man, I
ain't no Paki. But they was right man, they was right. They
know me better than I know myself. Paki. Nigel the Paki.
(*Again the contemptuous sound.*)

PHIL. You use that word a lot, Nige. You know that?

NIGEL. What? Paki?

PHIL. Yeah. You shouldn't be so racist.

NIGEL. Racist? You? Calling me racist? You, Babylon? You
fucking Stephen Lawrence killing Babylon?

PHIL. I'm just saying Nige. Some people find that kind of
language offensive, that's all

NIGEL. I tell you what's offensive. You the fucking offensive one
round here man. You, you cheap Armani seconds TK-Maxx
wearing cunt.

PHIL. Jesus Nigel, you really know where to hit where it hurts.

NIGEL. Well, what you expect? Calling me racist. I ain't no racist
see. I's fucking black, see. Black!

PHIL. Brown.

NIGEL. Black!

PHIL (*smiling*). So, you think that affected him? Finding out he
had a brother? That his father slept around?

NIGEL. Hey I don't know, copper. Ask him. Don't ask me. It
affected me, I'll tell you that, copper. It fucking affected me.

PHIL. I can see that.

NIGEL. What can you see? What can you see copper? You can't
see nothing!

NIGEL *feels unsteady on his feet, not well. He collapses
inside. His body searches for flatter ground – a chair, the floor.*

NIGEL. Hey look, I want to stop this now. All this secret spy shit.
It's draining me. I'm not well you know. I'm not well in the

head. I shouldn't have no pressure put on me. I's fucking borderline at best man. I gotta avoid shit that's gonna push me over that borderline.

PHIL. Aw come on Nigel, this is good. This is background. Deep background. You're doing good work here.

NIGEL. Am I shit. I can't stand no pressure man, they told me.

PHIL. Who told you?

NIGEL. Doctors man, doctors told me.

> PHIL *has prepared another drug-laced cigarette. He gives it to* NIGEL *almost surreptitiously.*

PHIL. Doctors? Doctors don't know shit, Nigel. This is a different border you're crossing now. Doctors don't know shit about what happens over here. Eh? You know what I'm talking about Nigel?

NIGEL. I told you.

PHIL. What've you told me. That he's a Paki? That's not news. Where is he? Where's he likely to go?

NIGEL. I don't know! That the only news I got. I went to his house. I went to . . . I don't know! I went everywhere. Nobody seen him. Nobody! Guy at the mosque said he remembered him but they ain't seen him since he went.

PHIL. Went where?

NIGEL. To study.

PHIL. Went where to study?

NIGEL. I don't know.

PHIL. Think Nigel, this is important.

NIGEL. I don't know, man. Yell-man or something.

PHIL. Yemen.

NIGEL. Yeah. Yell-man. Where's that?

PHIL. What was he doing there? Come on Nigel. What did he say?

NIGEL. Study, he say. Study! I told you, Karim, him a good bwa. Him study, see. Study, study, study. He probably a doctor out there now. Curing sick kids. That's the sort of thing he into, not blowing up planes.

PHIL. Who said anything about blowing up planes?

NIGEL. You did.

PHIL. No I didn't.

NIGEL. You did! I know what you want him for. You think
I don't, but I do. You think he's one of them guys . . . them
Empire State guys.

PHIL. What?

NIGEL. I saw the video, man . . . you know . . . (*Imitates a plane
flying into a building with his voice and his hands.*) You wrong
though. You wrong. I know that bwa. He's no killer. I's the
killer.

PHIL. Nigel . . .

NIGEL. No way that bwa's out there running like Billy the Kid,
man. No way.

PHIL. Nigel . . .

NIGEL *leans his head back and closes his eyes.* PHIL *gives up
on him, leaving him a minute, thinking.*

PHIL. Nigel. Nigel. Look lively.

NIGEL. You still here?

PHIL. Yeah. Which mosque did you go to?

NIGEL. Wha'?

PHIL. Which mosque did you go to?

NIGEL. I told you, man. I don't go to no mosque. I's English,
man.

PHIL. When you went looking for Karim? Which mosque did you
go to when you went looking for Karim?

NIGEL. Karim's mosque. The one up near the football.

PHIL. On Bentley Road?

NIGEL. Yeah.

PHIL. Did you go in?

NIGEL. Yeah. I told you. Nobody seen him since he went to what
do you call it . . . ?

PHIL. Yemen.

NIGEL. And that was four years ago man. That's it. The search is
over. Karim has gone to Yell-man and probably been a doctor
now.

PHIL. Yeah, that or a terrorist.

NIGEL. Terrorist? (*Giggles.*) You tripping man.

PHIL. I'm tripping?

NIGEL. Yeah, you tripping.

PHIL. I'm tripping?

NIGEL. Yeah. You tripping. I told you, man. It's all in your head.

PHIL. There's tanks at Heathrow airport, the whole country's shitting itself, your brother and a bunch of his mates are out there somewhere with a caseload of S.A.M. missiles looking to bag themselves a couple of Jumbo jets and you think it's all in my head! Do you know how many people are going to die if they shoot a fucking Jumbo jet down over London? Can you imagine what that's going to look like or sound like or smell like? Can you?

NIGEL. Hey, cool it man. Take a smoke.

PHIL. I don't want a smoke!

NIGEL. Fucking hell man . . . I thought we was going to chill.

PHIL. Aren't you fucking listening to me? Didn't you hear what I just said? People are going to die. Hundreds of people. Thousands of people. Don't you fucking care?

NIGEL. Yes! I care! Of course I care! It's just not my fault though! Is it? It's not my fault!

NIGEL *has crouched down with his arms protecting his head.*

PHIL. Nigel. Nigel. Come on now. You're right. It's not your fault.

NIGEL. That's what I've been trying to tell you.

PHIL. You're not your brother's keeper, right?

NIGEL. Right.

PHIL. You tried your best, you couldn't find him . . .

NIGEL. Yes. Right. See?

PHIL. Okay.

NIGEL. Okay.

PHIL. Okay. (*Pause.*) I'm sorry Nigel. I lost my temper there. I shouldn't have done that. I'm just under a lot of pressure, you know? A lot of stress . . .

NIGEL. Hey, I know stress. Don't let it get to you man. Stress is a killer. (*Tentatively, seeing* PHIL *prepare to leave*.) Is that it with us then? Are we cool?

PHIL. What? Yeah. We're cool.

NIGEL. You just going to leave?

PHIL. It was always going to be a long shot, wasn't it? You tried your best.

NIGEL. Yes. I did. I did try my best. .

NIGEL *begins to think his ordeal is over. He grows over-confident. He goes to the drugs on the table.*

NIGEL. Hey, you enjoy the rest of your day, officer, and if there's ever anything else I can help you with . . .

PHIL. Well, now that you mention it . . .

NIGEL. What? Oh no.

PHIL. It's nothing major, Nigel. I just need somebody to go inside that mosque for me.

NIGEL. What? No. No way.

PHIL. Come on Nige. you said if there was ever anything . . .

NIGEL. That's just one of them things you say man! It's like goodbye, you know? So let's say that shall we? Goodbye!

PHIL. Aw Nige.

NIGEL. I ain't doing it, man. I ain't going in no mosque. Them things give me the heebie-jeebies. I ain't doing it man. That is definitely not on anybody's agenda. No. No way. No!

PHIL. Okay.

NIGEL. What?

PHIL. Come on Nigel. If you don't want to do it I can't force you. It's still a free country, right?

NIGEL. Right.

PHIL. With laws and rights and things?

NIGEL. Yeah.

PHIL. It's what we're fighting for, after all. We give up on those we might as well just let them win. We'd be as bad as they are.

NIGEL. Yeah. Fuck. You had me going there. 'I need somebody to go in that mosque'. You got a sense of humour man. I like that.

It's quite dry, but I like it. We through then, you and me. we through?

PHIL. Yeah. Just one more thing. (PHIL *picks up the bags of drugs and puts them in an evidence bag*.) Nigel Brunswick, I'm arresting you for possession of Class 'A' drugs, you do not have to say anything, but anything you do say . . .

NIGEL. You gave me the drugs!

PHIL. Oh come on Nigel, you can do better than that. Even Helena Kennedy isn't going to buy that one.

NIGEL. But . . . but . . . you gave me the drugs!

PHIL. I'm a serving police officer Nigel. I wouldn't give anybody drugs. What happened was – Alerted by your erratic behaviour I executed a search of your person. In the course of that search it emerged you were carrying three and a half grams of heroin and a similar amount of cocaine packaged in seven separate wraps, ready for re-sale. On this evidence I deduced that you were not only a user but also quite possibly a supplier. A subsequent search of your domicile produced a further package of what seemed to be . . . (*He examines the package he has just taken from his pocket.*) Cocaine.

PHIL *tosses the package to* NIGEL, *who instinctively catches it, thus putting his fingerprints all over it.*

NIGEL. Oh man, you're evil.

PHIL. They're cracking down on dealers nowadays Nigel. You're not going to be seeing that Playstation of yours for a long, long time.

NIGEL. It's an X-box you loser.

PHIL (*cuffing* NIGEL). Yeah, yeah – tell it to the judge.

8.

That night. NIGEL *and* MARCO *are sitting around the stairwell playing cards. They are quiet and concentrated, playing card after card.*

NIGEL. Two threes.

MARCO. Two kings.

NIGEL. Three aces.

MARCO. Four kings.

NIGEL. Cheat! (MARCO *shows* NIGEL *his cards.*) Ah fuck! This
is a crap game.

MARCO. You suggested it.

NIGEL. Yeah well, don't ever listen to me. Any suggestion I ever
have is gonna be a pile of crap and the sooner you realise that
the sooner we can start . . . aw fuck I can't even remember
what I was gonna say half a second ago. This is crap.

MARCO. You all right Nigel?

NIGEL. Yeah. Fine. Just . . . I've got things on my mind, you
know.

MARCO. What sort of things?

NIGEL *shrugs dolefully. He is staring at the huge amount of
cards he has just picked up.*

Big things? Little things?

NIGEL (*throwing down cards*). Just fucking things, all right!

MARCO. Jesus Nige!

NIGEL. Ah wait, Marco . . . I'm sorry. I'm sorry man, it's just . . .

MARCO (*gathering cards*). You got things on your mind.

NIGEL. Yeah.

MARCO *has gathered the cards.* NIGEL *takes them, shuffles
them, deals.*

You ever wonder how you would handle it, Marco?

MARCO. What?

NIGEL. Doing time?

MARCO. Fucking hell Nigel, is that what you're thinking about.
Doing time?

NIGEL. Kinda.

MARCO. Why?

NIGEL. I don't know. I just got it into my head, you know? And
most of the things I get in my head stick there. I was just
wondering, you know, if it came to it . . . you think I could
do it?

MARCO. You ain't gonna do no time. You ain't a criminal.

NIGEL. No. I know. But it's a very subjective area that. Criminality. I ain't exactly got a blemish-free record, you know?

MARCO. You got arrested for pissing in a plant pot at the D.S.S., Nigel. Don't make you Ronnie Biggs.

NIGEL. I ain't saying I'm hardcore or nothing, I's just saying – could be one more stupid thing and the whole apparatus come down on me. Could be I'm looking at a long time, you know?

MARCO. Jesus Nigel, ain't gonna happen. Stop worrying.

NIGEL. But what if it did.

MARCO. This is super-cop, ain't it? He caught you with a tenner bag Nigel. That's a caution. No worries. It's not as if you're dealing or nothing, is it?

NIGEL *looks shifty.*

I said it's not as if you're dealing, Nigel?

NIGEL. Nah, course not. Nah. I was just wondering whether I could handle it or not. Hypothetically, you know? I did six months in that hospital.

MARCO. Prison ain't a hospital, Nigel. Prison's sposed to be rough. You playing this game?

NIGEL. Yeah. Four threes. I seen the movies, you know? Can't say I fancy it much.

MARCO. Two sevens.

NIGEL. Less it's a woman's prison, course. I fancy that very much. I fancy that very much if you know what I mean?

MARCO. Well, I hate to break it to you Nigel, but even a women's prison might be a bit too tough for you. If you know what I mean?

NIGEL. Says who?

MARCO. Aw come on, Nige. You gotta face it, man. You ain't hard.

NIGEL. Yeah I am.

MARCO. No you're not. You ain't no gangster, man. That's just that music you listen to. You ain't like that. They ain't even like that. All them rappers, man – they'd be squealing like bitches if

they ever had to go near a real jail. That Tupac was taking it up
the arse every night he was in there.

NIGEL. Hey, don't speak ill of the dead, man.

MARCO. No offence to the guy, Nigel, but he was. And even he's
harder than you. I tell you man. You gotta get those ideas out
of your head, or maybe you will end up in there. And really
man, that ain't somewhere you need to go. Are you playing
this?

NIGEL *sets down his cards.*

Nigel. Aw come on man. If you ain't going to play I'm going
home. Steve Irwin's on in ten. Nigel? Nigel? Christ Nigel, are
you crying?

NIGEL. No.

MARCO. You fucking are.

NIGEL. Leave me alone man, I ain't crying.

MARCO. Nigel.

NIGEL. Will you fucking leave it man. Go home watch your
fucking crocodile guy. I want to be on my own.

MARCO. Nigel. I ain't leaving you.

NIGEL. Go. Go on. I don't want you here. Don't you get that. I
don't want you here! What's wrong with you anyway? Why
you always hanging around me? You make me look like some
kind of batty boy kid fiddler the way you always hanging
round. What's the matter? Ain't you got any friends your own
age to play with?

MARCO *is cut to the core.*

MARCO. I got friends.

NIGEL. Well go and play with them then. Go on. Leave me I said.
I don't want you here no more!

MARCO. I'm going.

NIGEL. Good. And don't come near me again. I'm bad, man.
I am . . . I'm fucking . . . (*Clenches his fists, tenses his body.*)
Aw Marco . . . Marco man . . . I'm sorry man. Marco, you
come back here. Marco . . . (MARCO *holds up the palm of his
hand to him as he leaves.*) And don't be giving me none of that
talk-to-the-hand bullshit. You ain't on Jerry Springer now!
Marco! Shit!

PHIL *appears in the stairwell.*

PHIL. Problems?

NIGEL. What the fuck do you want?

PHIL *takes a seat on the stairs and smiles up at* NIGEL. NIGEL *goes after* MARCO.

Marco!

NIGEL *gives up on* MARCO. *His body slumps.*

PHIL. Well?

NIGEL. Well what?

PHIL. You made up your mind yet?

NIGEL. Yeah. I made up my mind.

PHIL. And?

NIGEL. And I'll see you fucking tomorrow, all right? Now fuck off and leave me alone. I want to be on my own, man. I want to be on my own.

PHIL *smirks contemptuously, gets up and leaves.* NIGEL *sits on the stairs and puts his head in his hands.* MRS MAC *is watching.*

9.

Next day. PHIL *waits in* NIGEL*'s living room. There are a pile of CDs lying around.* PHIL *leafs through them.*

PHIL. Ja Rule, Beanie Man, the Notorious B.I.G . . . Isn't it time you stopped listening to this shit and got yourself a job?

NIGEL *pops his head round the door.*

NIGEL. What's that?

PHIL. This shit. (*He tosses CD aside with contempt.*) I said isn't it about time you stopped listening to this shit and got yourself a job.

NIGEL. Ain't you heard copper. I's mental. I don't ever have to work ever again.

PHIL. And you think that's a good thing, do you?

NIGEL. What? You don't?

PHIL. No.

NIGEL. I don't know man. I been doing this for several years now and I ain't found no downside yet.

PHIL. Christ Nigel. Don't you want to do something with your life?

NIGEL. I's doing it.

PHIL. I give up.

NIGEL. What? You think I should get all respectable now I's joined the police force.

PHIL. Nigel . . .

NIGEL. What?

PHIL. You haven't . . . oh nothing. Forget it. How long are you going to be in there? What are you doing anyway?

NIGEL. Hey, you want me to look my best, don't you?

PHIL. I don't care, I just want this thing done.

NIGEL. Me too. Just give me one more second man, I want to get this just right. Okay. You ready?

PHIL. Yeah.

NIGEL. Close your eyes.

PHIL. What?

NIGEL. Close your eyes.

PHIL. Christ . . .

NIGEL. They closed yet?

PHIL. Yes.

NIGEL *peeps out again, checking* PHIL*'s eyes are closed. He comes out. He is wearing a long Moslem-style suit or robe beneath a camouflage flak jacket, topped off with a little Moslem style hat and mirror shades.*

NIGEL. Ta da!

PHIL (*opening his eyes*). Fucking hell.

NIGEL. You like?

PHIL. No I do not fucking like. What are you playing at? You're supposed to be some disturbed misfit, not a fucking Mujahadin tank commander.

NIGEL. Hey, if I's going undercover I want to look the part.

PHIL. You twat. Where did you get that stuff?

NIGEL. The hat and the shades and the jacket – they's mine. This neat little suit man, I found it, found it out the back.

PHIL. You found it?

NIGEL. Yeah man. I found it. It was hanging off some rope out the back.

PHIL. Rope? What? You mean a clothes line?

NIGEL. Kinda.

PHIL. Jesus Nigel, the amount of police time that gets wasted every year chasing after the perverts and nut jobs who thieve people's washing . . . There'll be some old dear getting mugged down the precinct right now because the coppers who are supposed to be patrolling it are too busy reassuring some housewife that there's every chance her old man'll get his best holiday suit back.

NIGEL. Chaos theory, cool.

PHIL. I'm not talking about chaos theory, I'm talking about you thieving.

NIGEL. What? You think they was gonna come and get it back?

PHIL. Christ Nigel. I think you do this deliberately.

NIGEL. Course I do, Columbo. I got it off Oxfam years ago. Just liked the colour. You really thought I was going to turn up at the mosque dressed like this. Sucker. I ain't mad. Well, I am, but not that mad. I was just joshing with you man. Thought it would break the tension. Obviously not.

PHIL. Are you going to come here and look at these pictures?

NIGEL. What pictures?

PHIL. These are the guys you need to look out for. They're all regulars. Now this one . . .

NIGEL. Oh man, he ugly!

PHIL. Burned his face in Afghanistan. First time round.

NIGEL. First time round what? (PHIL's *face blackens*.) Hey relax, I'm playing with you. I know about Afghanni-stan.

PHIL (*grabbing* NIGEL). You are not going to fuck this up Nigel. You hear me? This might be some big fucking joke to you but my career is riding on this. These are serious fucking people, Nigel. They've done shit you can't even imagine. Now come here and look at these pictures. Look at them.

PHIL *is pushing* NIGEL*'s face into the photos, his reply is muffled.*

NIGEL. Hey! Ain't no joke to me neither.

PHIL. What?

NIGEL. I said it ain't no joke to me neither, man. I'm fucking bricking it. You think I want to play secret squirrel in some fucking mosque man? You think that's my idea of a boombastic jazz tune? You should fucking lighten up man. My arse is on the line here. What if they suss me?

PHIL. How are they going to suss you?

NIGEL. Well for one thing I could just walk in there and go – Hi, I'm Nigel, I'm here to spy on you – could one of you kind gentlemen please direct me to where them bad motherfuckers are at?

PHIL. And why would you do that?

NIGEL. I don't know man. I got Tourettes. I don't know what's gonna come out of my mouth from one moment to the next.

PHIL. That's not Tourettes Nigel. That's just you being a stupid cunt.

NIGEL. As long as we got that cleared up. What if they suss me though? I'm serious. I ain't equipped to deal with that shit.

PHIL. You'll be fine, Nigel. Trust me. You don't have to do anything. You just go in, take a look around, pick up a leaflet, read through it. Somebody's going to come up to you and say – 'Is this your first time here?' or 'I haven't seen you here before' or 'Can I help you sir'. All you've got to say is 'Yes'. You tell them you've passed the place a lot. You always wondered what it was like inside. You felt the need for some peace and quiet. They'll take it from there. All you've got to do is be cool, Nige. Just be cool.

NIGEL. Like Fonzie?

PHIL. Yeah, like Fonzie. Trust me, Nigel. You're going to be okay.

At this point no one in the room believes this to be true.

10.

MRS MAC *has been snooping at her door. She closes the door and comes back inside. She potters about, talking to the picture of her dead husband, Harry.*

MRS MAC. He's down there again, Harry. That policeman.
There's something fishy going on there, I can tell you.
Policeman. I'll policeman him. I think I can spot a queer
shilling at my age. What's that? No, you're right. I never
spotted Nigel. But Nigel always seemed such a nice boy.
Feckless, of course, but nice you know . . . always very polite.
You can tell a lot about people by their manners. Hmm. No,
you're right. They would train them to be polite. That's how
they do it, isn't it? Their modus operandi. Find a nice quiet
little stair. Keep their heads down. Be polite. Nodding, smiling.
And all the time, all the time they're . . . Oh, it doesn't bear
thinking about. You know, I never had much time for the
Germans, but at least you could see them coming. Hear them,
anyway. Those engines, God. That was terrible Harry, terrible
times. We thought all that was behind us, didn't we? The
bombs, the fires. Fifth columnists. Careless talk costs lives.
Remember those first few months? Spies everywhere, or so we
thought. Yes, you're right. I think in retrospect Mannie
Schwartzkopf was just a butcher. I don't think he was even
German to tell you the truth. Still. Didn't stop his window
getting panned in. It was not my brother. Oh well, maybe it
was. Always very . . . what's the word . . . pro-active. Yes, very
pro-active our Billy. Very patriotic too. Always on the look out
for Catholics. I used to tell him, Billy, we live in Bridgeton,
we're surrounded by Catholics. Didn't stop him chasing them
though, did it? Didn't stop him getting killed. Monte Cassino.
Where the fudge is Monte Cassino? Yes, I know it's in Italy, I
was being . . . thingy, you know . . . rhetorical. Poor Billy. Yes,
poor Mannie Schwartzkopf too. I think he's down here now,
you know. I heard he'd settled here. Yes, you're right. He will
be dead by now. He made lovely sausages, Manny.

So, do you think . . . No, it's too much. Nigel isn't a terrorist.
How could he be? He can't even lace his shoes up properly,
poor mite. And he's always got his stair money ready. Don't
have to chase him up. Not like that trollop upstairs. He is very
dark though. Pakistani that policeman says. Doesn't smell like
a Pakistani. Do you remember that family? Course you do?
On Balfour Street? Every time you passed the door there'd be

this smell. Yes, I know it was curry. I know that now. But at
the time? God, we had no idea what it was. They could've
been boiling cats for all we knew. Yes, I know. Don't keep
interrupting me. No, I don't know exactly how hard it is to
catch a cat, I do know it's a lot easier just to go to the butchers
and get a bit of lamb. It was a long time ago Harry. We weren't
so au fait then with unfamiliar cuisine. Mince and tatties.
Mince and tatties don't smell. Oh no, he couldn't be. Not
Nigel. You go have a look. I'm not worried. It takes more than
that to frighten me, my lad. I've still got the key, of course.
Mrs Ingersol's. I could just pop down. Have a look. Of course
I know what a bomb looks like. What's that? No, she was
Norwegian, poor soul.

I never had the chance to, Harry. They just came in and
emptied the place. All her bags, all her belongings, out into the
skip. It's a terrible thing dying alone, Harry. A terrible thing.
I'm so lucky I've still got you. Will we watch TV? Oh look,
it's that fat one. How did she get on TV, the trollop?

11.

PHIL *waits for* NIGEL *at the swings. He is pacing, agitated,*
looking at his watch. He sees NIGEL *approaching and goes to*
him, eager to hear how it went. NIGEL *is not in the best of moods*
and does not stop for him.

PHIL. Well, did you do it?

NIGEL. Yeah, I did it.

PHIL. Well? What did you say?

NIGEL. What do you think I said?

PHIL. With you Nige, it's hard to tell.

NIGEL. I told them the fucking truth, man!

PHIL. You wh? Jesus . . .

NIGEL. I told them the truth! I'm a young man who don't fit in
    nowhere, who gets picked on cause of the colour of his skin,
    who gets harassed by Babylon night and day for no fucking
    reason man, who's carrying the bruises of police brutality, who
    just wants a bit of peace an' quiet but can't get none, who gets

so het up by uncompromising white authority he wants to get a gun and start shooting and shooting and shooting! And man, that is the truth. I do want to shoot man. I want to shoot you. I want to shoot your wife. I want to blow up your whole fucking world man. I hate you.

PHIL. You said that?

NIGEL. Yeah, I said that.

PHIL. That's fucking brilliant, Nigel.

NIGEL. What? How's that brilliant?

PHIL. It's a touch of fucking genius. I knew I was on to something with you.

NIGEL. What? Tell me? How can that be brilliant? How can that be good in any way, man? Less than a month ago I was happy. I had my spliff, my TV, my x-box. I was happy, man. I was living the dream. Now look at me? I want to kill people. How can that be good?

PHIL. Trust me, Nigel, it's good.

NIGEL. Trust me Nigel it's fucking fucked up and it's all down to you.

PHIL. So what did he say? When you told him that?

NIGEL. He told me I needed guidance. Too right I need guidance. I don't know who I am anymore.

PHIL. Is that all?

NIGEL. He told me to come to this meeting. What's it called? (*He pulls a flyer out of his pocket.*) 'Principles of Jihad-the holy warrior and the secular state'.

PHIL. Oh fuck, don't tell me that.

NIGEL. Why? Is that bad?

PHIL. No, that's brilliant, Nigel. I just about creamed myself there. You are getting me hot boy!

NIGEL. Hey look, I ain't no fairy, all right.

PHIL. Yeah, yeah, stop being so literal now. He actually invited you along to a meeting called that?

NIGEL. Yeah.

PHIL. And you said?

NIGEL. What you think I said? I said – yeah, I played that game before. Got to the second level.

PHIL. You said what? No. What did he say?

NIGEL. He didn't say nothing. He just look at me. Yeah. The way you're looking at me now. Then he say – 'This isn't a game, boy'. Yeah, that's what he said. So I said 'Chill, it's a joke. English humour man. I know what Jihad is'. Hey, and get this. I said to him right, I said to him . . . 'I have always felt myself to have a warrior's soul. The frustrations of my life come from this. From being a warrior in a time of no war'.

PHIL. Fucking hell Nigel. Did you make that up?

NIGEL. What? No. It was in a comic. X-men or something.

PHIL. You amaze me.

NIGEL. Yeah. You amaze me too. I guess we're just a couple of amazing guys.

PHIL. So you're going?

NIGEL. Yeah. I'm going.

PHIL. I'm going to get you a wire.

NIGEL. No you're not.

PHIL. Yes I am. And you're going to wear it. It's tiny Nigel, trust me.

NIGEL. Will you stop fucking saying that. It really does something to my dignity when you say 'Trust me' and I'm s'posed to nod my head. I ain't never gonna trust you man. You is a serpent man, you is a snake, and even I is nowhere near mad enough to trust a snake.

PHIL. Okay, don't trust me. Do as I say.

NIGEL. That's what I'm fucking doing man. But I ain't trusting you, and I ain't pretending to no more. Fuck it. Ain't you scared, man?

PHIL. Scared of what?

NIGEL. Scared I's gonna go over. Scared I's gonna actually be like one of them.

PHIL. Christ Nigel – you're way too lazy to be one of them.

NIGEL. What?

PHIL. It's a tough, disciplined life being a Mujahadin, Nigel. You're not tough and you're not disciplined.

NIGEL. Oh yeah? And what am I?

PHIL. You're just another lazy, unfocussed dole boy who thinks sitting around in his underwear watching 'This Morning' with Fern and Phillip is a satisfactory way to spend his life.

NIGEL. What do you know?

PHIL. I know they don't show fucking 'Countdown' on Al-Jazeera. Come on Nigel. I know what you are. You know what you are. Let's not say it out loud, eh?

NIGEL. No. So what am I?

PHIL. I told you.

NIGEL. So what am I? Tell me? Say it out loud?

PHIL. Nigel, you're a loser. Live with it, okay?

NIGEL. Hey. Hey. If I'm a loser what does that make you?

PHIL. Think about it Nigel. Think before you open your mouth. (*In phone.*) Yeah, look, it's Phil. I need some of that equipment the Super was talking about, the buttonhole stuff. The fibre optics.

NIGEL. I ain't wearing no wire, man!

PHIL *waves* NIGEL *away.* NIGEL *takes a few steps, turns back, is about to say something.* PHIL *waves him away again.* NIGEL *departs, frustrated.*

PHIL. Yeah, I know it's not authorised but I'm on to something. Remember that guy I told you about? Yeah. I got him inside. Yeah, he's in there. Yeah, I know. I told you, didn't I? We'll bust that mosque wide open while Special Branch are still scratching their arses. Yeah, I thought you'd like the sound of that. We pull this off and the sky's the limit. Hey, if you want a blow job off Blunkett I'm sure that could be arranged. And I'll be right there beside you, mate, snorting coke off Tony's fat, spotty arse. Yeah, couple of heroes, mate. Yeah. Typical, ain't it – a billion dollars' worth of spy planes and it's still the humble British bobby who gets the results. You just get me that wire, mate. I'll take care of the rest.

12.

NIGEL *is returning home, pissed off with the world but especially the six or so square feet of it inhabited by* PHIL.

NIGEL. Loser? Who he calling a fucking loser, man? I'll show him. I'll get his fucking balls and put them in a vice, man – I'll squeeze them til they burst man. I'll shove red hot needles up his arse man, see who's a fucking loser then. Like he fucking knows. Bastard!

He sees a flash of light in the stairwell. MARCO *is hiding there and has just lit a cigarette.* NIGEL *adopts a hunting position. He edges slowly towards the stairwell. He picks up a half brick that is lying around to use as a weapon. He holds it above his head as he edges forward.*

Who's that? Who's there? Karim?

MARCO *moves and* NIGEL *sees his face.*

Marco! Jesus, man. I thought that fucking brother of mine had turned up. That copper's got me wrong in the fucking head again. I tell you man, any day now I'm going to start hearing them dogs talking to me again, man. You hear me man?

MARCO *ignores him.*

So what? You ain't talking to me, is that it? If this about all that stuff last night you know I don't mean none of that, don't you? It's that fucking copper man, he's got me so wound up I don't know if I'm shitting or farting. You know what I mean? Marco . . .? Marco! Will you fucking talk to me!

MARCO. Leave me alone, will you!

MARCO *is upset and has been crying. He goes to get past* NIGEL. NIGEL *hauls him back.*

NIGEL. Marco. Come on, man. I'm your best friend, man. Don't get like that.

MARCO. Leave me alone!

NIGEL. Marco! I ain't letting you past til you . . . .

MARCO. Where were you man? Where were you? Where were you? Where were you? Where were you?

MARCO *pummels* NIGEL *with his fists, tears filling his eyes.* NIGEL *sees he has been badly beaten.*

NIGEL. Marco? Marco man? What happened to you?

MARCO. Nothing. Just let me past.

NIGEL. Fuck nothing. You got blood all over you man. Who did this to you? Who did this? Tell me?

MARCO. Nobody!

NIGEL. You tell me, Marco. I ain't having this. I ain't having nobody hitting you.

MARCO. Nige, forget it, eh?

NIGEL. Ain't gonna forget it. Somebody attack my friend they attack me. I'll fucking get them man. I'll kill them. I know you think I'm some sort of pussy get his head kickin in a women's prison, but I's serious. I kill whoever did this to you with a bat, man. I'll hit home runs off their fucking head man.

MARCO *is by now both crying and laughing.*

What? You think I won't? You think old Nigel ain't gangster enough for them?

MARCO. Christ, Nigel . . . I know you will. I know you kill them, man.

NIGEL. Too right I kill them. I don't want no one beating on you, Marco. You my friend, man. Ain't nobody hit my friend.

MARCO. Can I stay with you tonight, Nige.

NIGEL. Sure you can. You can stay any time you want. Don't you want to get back to your mum, though. Need a woman to patch up this shit.

MARCO. Nah. I don't want to go back there.

NIGEL. What? Why not? She ain't gonna be mad with you. Ain't your fault you got beat up.

MARCO. Let's just go to yours, eh? Please Nigel . . .

NIGEL. Oh wait? Was this one of her blokes? Was it?

MARCO. Ain't none of her blokes.

NIGEL. Who then? What's wrong, Marco? Why don't you want to . . . Oh fuck, Marco . . . look at your back man. (*There are thin lines of blood seeping through* MARCO*'s white T-shirt*) Who did this? Oh shit. She did this to you, didn't she? Didn't she? That fucking slut did this to you!

MARCO. No. Nigel, wait . . . It was my own fault.

NIGEL. Your own fault? What? You bang yourself again? You bang yourself on the head and on the ribs and . . . let's look at that . . . (*He pulls T-shirt up his back.*) Oh shit. What? You told her take a fucking coat-hanger to your back like that?

MARCO. It was my own fault Nigel.

NIGEL. No. It was not your fault. I do not care what you did to her or said to her she ain't got no right to treat you like that. You're just a kid, man. Nobody's got the right to go hitting kids.

MARCO. I ain't no kid.

NIGEL. You fucking are, Marco. You're fifteen years old. That makes you a kid no matter how tough you think you are. And that makes you off limits when the fucking coat-hangers start flying. She's your mother man, ain't your fucking pimp. You don't need that sort of shit in your life.

MARCO. She's me mum, Nige.

NIGEL. Well she should act like your fucking mum. Ain't you watch TV? Ain't you ever seen the fucking Waltons, man? You ever see fat mama Walton take a coat-hanger to John Boy or Sue Ellen? No. She fucking loves them, man. She supports them. She ain't turning no tricks in the next room while her kids are trying to master the intricacies of play station fucking two.

MARCO *starts crying again.*

Aw come on Marco, don't cry man. I's just saying. This fucked-up thing don't have to happen. You stop blaming yourself, eh? If your mother ain't no fit human being that ain't your fault. You the coolest guy I know man. You always smiling, no matter what shit you going through. You're smart, you go to school. I tell you man, one day you're gonna get some well fuck-off job, and you gonna be coming through here swanning man – you gonna have one o' them black Golf Gti's man, with the roof down and the tinted windows, you're gonna be Moschino head to foot man, you are . . . And you're gonna cruise around the fucking streets waving man . . . You're gonna show them what a good man can get for his self without even resorting to crime. I can't wait. I can't wait til you show them, man. And you will show them. Cause you're smart man, and you're good, and if that bitch can't see it man, don't matter if she is your mother, you gotta cut her out of your life.

MARCO. Is that what you did?

NIGEL. Me?

MARCO. With your mum?

NIGEL. My mum? Jesus Marco . . . I didn't have the chance. My mum can't bear to fucking look at me, and I don't blame her. She's got the right. You don't know what I was like when I was eighteen man. I was mad, just straight mad. I was hearing voices and seeing things and all sorts. I was accusing her of trying to kill me – I thought she was sending agents after me. That's why my mum can't bear to look at me. I gave her reasons. Okay, so I was ill. But you can't just expect somebody to forget shit like that just because the pills are maybe working. But you? You, man? All you ever did to your mother was look out for her like a good boy. And you are a good boy. You don't deserve no coat-hanger beatings. You don't deserve your back to look like that.

MARCO. I wind her up, Nigel. I do.

NIGEL. You fucking don't. And I'll tell you something else. You keep talking like that and I'm personally gonna march you on 'Trisha' and get her to sort out your arse. I ain't having none of that low self-esteem crap around you Marco, cause you're a fucking good kid. You're cool man. You're cool as a goose.

MARCO. A what?

NIGEL. What? You never see a goose before? You don't think they cool?

MARCO. I don't know Nige. Ducks are cool.

NIGE L. And what is a goose but a big fucking duck? A goose is the biggest, hardest duck in the whole fucking world man. Come on now, dry your eye, you're coming home with me. Ain't nobody gonna hit you any more, seen?

13.

NIGEL's flat. NIGEL lies on the floor reading. MARCO comes in in his pyjamas, carrying a cup of tea.

MARCO. What's that you're reading?

NIGEL. This book I got from a guy down the mosque.

MARCO. Christ Nigel, you're not reading the Koran are you.

NIGEL. Nah. This one begins with a Q or something. It's sorta poetry. Poetry about God.

MARCO. Jesus Nigel, that is the . . . (NIGEL *looks up at him.*) forget it, doesn't matter . . .

NIGEL. It's good.

MARCO. Yeah. I heard. (*Pause.*) Christ Nigel, I don't like you going down there. It's dangerous. You should tell super-cop to shove it. He can't force you.

NIGEL. I ain't going there for super-cop. I like it there. It's peaceful.

MARCO. You're still reporting back to him though, ain't you?

NIGEL. What's to report? Bunch of old guys come in and take their shoes off. Big deal. Officer Phil is off his fucked-up little head.

MARCO. He has got a little head, hasn't he?

NIGEL. Yeah. Tiny little head. He's still a psycho though. I'd better go. You gonna be all right in here?

MARCO. Yeah. Got everything thanks. Okay if I take a bath?

NIGEL. Knock yourself out, little buddy. I gotta dash. (*Stops at door.*) You ain't seen Mrs Mac lately, have you?

MARCO. Who?

NIGEL. Old biddy lives upstairs.

MARCO. Nah.

NIGEL. Hope she's all right. I'll maybe go up and look when I get back. Check there ain't a pile of papers and milk bottles and what not. Hope she's okay.

> NIGEL *leaves.* MRS MAC *comes to the door and watches him leave. She goes back inside. Cross fade to* MRS MAC*'s flat.*

MRS MAC. He's gone. I'd better go now if I'm going to. No. Cup of tea first. Cup of tea to steady my nerves.

> MRS MAC *puts a kettle on the gas.*

> Terrorists. Imagine it? We're not safe in our own homes, Harry. Yes, you're right. If I'm going to go I should go now. He might come back, and then where will I be? But what if he is hiding the brother? He's a murderer that policeman said. I'll take a poker. That'll sort him out.

Cross fade again. MRS MAC *creeps stealthily towards*
NIGEL'*s door, poker in hand. She bends down and looks
through the letterbox. Nothing. She goes in her pocket for Mrs
Ingersol's key. She opens the door. Cross fade –* NIGEL'*s flat.*
MRS MAC *enters the flat with the same stealth she
approached the door. What is she looking for? Now she's in
she's not so sure.*

Now then?

She sees a drawer and opens it, begins looking through.
MARCO *comes out of the bathroom with a towel wrapped
round his waist.*

MARCO. What the . . .

MARCO *eyes up the intruder. Circles stealthily.*

Can I help you?

MRS MAC. Aaagh!

MARCO. What the . . .

MRS MAC. Get back! I'm armed!

MARCO. Who the fuck are you?

MRS MAC. Who are you, more to the point? This is Nigel's flat
you know?

MARCO. Yeah.

MRS MAC. You're him, aren't you?

MARCO. Who?

MRS MAC. Him. The brother.

MARCO. Look, if that's some racial thing I really gotta say
I don't like it.

MRS MAC. Keep back. I'll phone the police.

MARCO. Phone them. You're the burglar.

MRS MAC. I most certainly am not.

MARCO. You most certainly are so. Just cause you're a fucking
wrinkly don't mean you can just come in people's houses, you
know? I don't care how poxy your pension is, theft's theft.

MRS MAC. I'm no thief.

MARCO. You fucking are.

MRS MAC. Oh! That's it. I'm phoning the police.

MARCO. Phone them. I'll tell you what – if you won't phone them I will. I'm sick of this shit.

MRS MAC (*raising poker*). Keep back!

MRS MAC *aims the poker at* MARCO*'s head.* MARCO *jumps back. His towel falls.* NIGEL *walks in.*

NIGEL. I just forgot my . . . fucking hell.

MRS MAC. Aaaagh!

NIGEL. Marco? Mrs Mac? I don't fucking believe this. She's fucking ancient Marco. She's at least eighty five. And you, shame on you Mrs McCallum. He's just a boy. He's fifteen years old for fuck sake. That's fucking jailbait, you know?

MARCO. I ain't shagging her, Nigel. She's robbing the fucking gaff.

MRS MAC. I most certainly am not.

MARCO. Then what you doing here?

MRS MAC. Oh! Oh! I was looking for bombs!

NIGEL. Bombs?

MARCO. Bombs?

MRS MAC. Yes. Bombs. He said you were a terrorist. He said you were plotting against the state. He said we were all in very grave danger.

NIGEL. Who did?

MRS MAC. Who? Him. The policeman.

MARCO. Fucking hell.

NIGEL. You mean Super-cop? Officer Phil? That skinny cunt in the secondhand suit?

MRS MAC. Yes. He said you were conspiring.

NIGEL. Conspiring?

MRS MAC. Conspiring with enemies of the state. Terrorists. He said to keep my eyes open for a Paki . . . stani . . . a Pakistani with a beard.

MARCO. Do I look like a fucking Pakistani?

MRS MAC. He said he was a master of disguise.

NIGEL. Jesus fucking Christ. I do not believe that guy.

MARCO *is pissing himself laughing.*

MRS MAC. So you're not a terrorist?

NIGEL. No. It's me, Mrs Mac. Nigel. I's lived here six years. I's talked to you just about every single fucking day of them six years. I've made cups of fucking tea for you, you batty old slag, and some cunt comes along and calls me a terrorist and you just fucking believe him. This is too much.

MRS MAC. Oh Nigel . . .

NIGEL. And to top it off you come in my house. You break in my house. What kind of person breaks into somebody's house? What the fuck is wrong with all you white people? Why the fuck do you keep coming into my house? And you can stop laughing too you cunt!

MRS MAC. Oh Nigel, I'm so sorry. You're right. You've been a really good neighbour to me. I can't believe I listened to him. But I was scared. It's on the news every night you know. Terrorists here, terrorists there. I haven't been sleeping, Nigel.

NIGEL. You think I have. That man, Mrs Mac, that policeman is a fiend. He's blackmailing me. He planted drugs on me, you know? He says you help me or I'm putting you in jail. He's making my life an absolute fucking misery, pardon my French, and all because he's got it into his head that my half brother who I haven't seen in seven years is some kind of international terrorist mastermind. I wouldn't care but I don't even know the geezer. I ain't seen him since he was sixteen.

MRS MAC. Oh Nigel. I'm sorry, Can you forgive me.

NIGEL. Yeah. Course. No wait, how'd you get in?

MRS MAC. I've got a key. Mrs Ingersol's . . .

NIGEL. Who?

MRS MAC. Mrs Ingersol. She lived here before you. She died here actually. Right here. Well over there, actually. There where your friend is sitting.

MARCO *jumps up and looks with disgust at the space he has just vacated. He starts brushing his backside, as if he'd sat in something disgusting.*

NIGEL. Ah God . . . look, just give me the key, yeah. Give me the key and we'll forget this ever happened. But I'm not a terrorist, right?

MRS MAC. No Nigel, of course not. I'm sorry.

NIGEL. No harm done, yeah?

MRS MAC. Thank you Nigel. You're very understanding.

NIGEL. Mrs McCallum . . . wait . . .

MRS MAC. Yes?

NIGEL. That's the stair money sitting there. You never came to collect it this week.

MRS MAC. Oh.

MRS MAC *sheepishly picks up the money and retires.*

NIGEL. Silly mare. Terrorists? Jesus? What did she think I was going to do?

MRS MAC *can be seen outside her front door, about to light a cigarette. As she goes inside* Nigel *says –*

Blow up her flat?

A huge explosion rips across the stage. NIGEL and MARCO are flung to the ground. They get to their feet. They head towards the door, moving gingerly. They look outside. MRS MAC is standing in the stairs in a state of shock. Her clothes and face are blackened. Her cigarette is still in her mouth. The end of the cigarette is frazzled.

14.

The Swings. NIGEL waits. PHIL comes up and sits on the swing next to him. He is eating chips.

PHIL. Chip?

NIGEL *shakes his head.*

Suit yourself?

He takes one last chip, bundles up the rest and throws them away.

NIGEL. Aw man, you don't need to litter, you know?

PHIL. What? It's biodegradable. Nice treat for the rats. Or don't you think rats should have any perks. I mean talking as a rat.

NIGEL. I ain't a rat, man.

PHIL. Nah, course not. You're a valuable resource, Nigel. Besides, even a rat wouldn't be seen dead in a hat like that.

NIGEL *takes off his hat and hides it away, looking resentfully towards* PHIL.

PHIL. So, I heard you had a bit of trouble last week?

NIGEL. What trouble?

PHIL. The old bird up stairs?

NIGEL. Oh, Mrs Mac. Yeah. She blew herself up, man. Gas.

PHIL. She all right then? Or are you still scraping her tits off the walls?

NIGEL. Aah man, that's horrible. Nah, she's okay. I think she shit herself like. And I don't mean hypothetically. She staying with me now. Til she gets her flat sorted.

PHIL. With you?

NIGEL. Yeah. Why not? We's neighbours ain't we? She ain't got nobody else.

PHIL. Yeah, I mean, but . . . with you?

NIGEL. Yeah, with me. She needed help so I's helping her, okay? That's what good people do, man.

PHIL. And you're one of the good people now, are you?

NIGEL *shrugs*

Still, must be a bit of a drag, having an old woman around all the time?

NIGEL. She's okay. She was telling me about the war, man. Unbelievable. You know that woman almost got killed twenty-seven times, man. And that was just in 1940. That's real Bruce Willis stuff, man. Serious Die Hard. Us young people, we don't know we're born man.

PHIL. I've got to admit, when the call first came through I thought that brother of yours had turned up. Amazing how often these homemade bomb factories blow up in your face, just when you're least expecting it.

NIGEL. Yeah well, sorry to disappoint you.

PHIL. I'm not disappointed, Nigel. He'll turn up.

NIGEL. Ain't this where you say – 'His type always do'?

PHIL. Yeah. His type always do. So, what you got for me? Chemical warfare suits in the broom cupboard? 'I love Osama' coffee mugs on sale in the foyer? 'My boyfriend went to Afghanistan and all he brought me back was this lousy prayer mat' prayer mats . . . ? Anything like that . . . Come on, Nige, I'm having a shit day here, help me out. Nigel? You listening to me?

NIGEL. Yeah. I'm listening. I'm listening, man. Look, ain't being funny or nothing, but have you actually got anything on him? I mean, you just think he's bad, or you got proof on him?

PHIL. Who? Karim? Nigel, sweet little Karim has got a warrant out on him in three different countries. He's definitely bad.

NIGEL. Karim?

PHIL. Yes, Karim. Jesus Nigel, what is it with you? Have you just not been paying attention or something? What do you think the last few months of your life have been all about?

NIGEL. I don't know man, I just thought maybe you was a bit paranoid or something. I seen a lot of that you know?

PHIL. Yeah well, tell that to the mother of the baby his last bomb killed.

NIGEL. What? You serious? A baby?

PHIL. Look Nige, I know you're having a bit of trouble getting your head round all this, but we've got a trail on Karim going back to 1998. We can connect him to gangs in Germany, France and Morocco. We've got his prints all over the kitchen of a bomb factory in Lyon. And now we're right back where it all started. The Bentley Road Mosque. They took that kid when he was confused and vulnerable and turned him into a baby killing terrorist. And that's where we come in. Because we're going to get the guys who did that to Karim. And we're going to get Karim too, if we get the chance, because he's got the taste for it now, and once they get the taste there's no going back. We clear with that, Nigel? It's not a game. This is the real world now. People are dying.

NIGEL. A baby? Man, you better not be making this up.

PHIL. I'm not making it up, Nigel.

NIGEL. I ain't seen nothing like that going on in there.

PHIL. What have you seen?

NIGEL. I don't know. Good people, man. Good people. There's this old guy there, Ahmed right, I sit with him sometimes. He was telling me all about this place he's from. Algeria. Sounds cool man. They's all followers of Allah there, man. God fearing people.

PHIL. Yeah, I suppose that's why we keep arresting them all. What about Al-Answari? The one with the scars? You seen him any?

NIGEL. Yeah, I seen him.

PHIL. Talk to him?

NIGEL (*shrugs*). Some.

PHIL (*pause*). And?

NIGEL. And nothing, man. The guy creep me out. Every time I see him coming I get a desperate need for a jimmy, man.

PHIL. He's the one you're targeting.

NIGEL. He's the one targeting me. That bug-eyed stare man, always looking at me. I think he's one of them, you know?

PHIL. What? Al-Qaeda?

NIGEL. No. One of them. A hoofter, man.

PHIL. Fuck sake, Nigel. The guy's got a hundred kids.

NIGEL. I don't care how many kids he got man, them fucking Arabs is weird. They don't care what they eat, man. They's as happy with Linda MacCartney as they is with Ronald MacDonald's.

PHIL. He's not a queer, Nigel, trust me on that. Look, next time you see him I want you to talk to him. You tell him – I don't know – tell him your brother used to come to this mosque. Tell him he got the chance to go to Yemen to study. Tell him you'd like to visit that part of the world too some day. Tell him all that shit about how you're a young black man who doesn't know where he belongs. That's like 'Open Sesame' to those cunts. And record it, okay? I want every word he says.

NIGEL. Ah. I was meaning to talk to you about that.

PHIL. What?

NIGEL. It's this wire, man. I don't think it's working no more.

NIGEL *takes out the wire. It looks rather forlorn. There are crusted pieces of pink toilet tissue stuck to it.*

PHIL. Nigel? What did you do? (*With mounting alarm.*) What did you do?

NIGEL. I don't know, man. I forgot it was there. I had to go for a dump man. I forgot it was down me trousers. It fell . . .

PHIL. Jesus Nigel! Do you know how much that cost. I'm not even supposed to have it for fuck sake!

NIGEL. It ain't my fault man. I told you I didn't want to use it.

PHIL. Christ, I've had enough of this.

NIGEL. What you gonna do?

PHIL. I don't know. Okay. First off I'm going to take this back where it came from and get it cleaned up.

NIGEL. Yeah. I think that's a good idea.

PHIL. Then I'm going to take it back to you and personally strap it into place. I'm going to march you down to that mosque and watch you go in the front door. And I'm going to be listening, okay? Every step of the way. You're going to find Al-Answari. You're going to follow his every step. Every time that cunt turns round he's going to be looking at you. You're Karim's brother, Nigel – you're a Jihadi, a martyr in the making. You're going to let him know how much you hate white authority. You're going to let him know you're prepared to do whatever it takes to make the great Satan scream. And you're going to stay there, getting deeper and deeper, until I've got something I can go to my bosses with, until we finally get that one thing we need to go in there with all guns blazing. You got that?

NIGEL. I don't know if I can do this, Phil.

PHIL. What do you mean? You're going to do it.

NIGEL. I can't, man. I can't. Going to that mosque was the best thing ever happened to me. I ain't scared no more, see. I got this feeling in me, man . . . I's peaceful, man, peaceful. I ain't giving that up for no one. I'm sorry man. I ain't going to do this no more.

PHIL. I told you what would happen to you if you bottled this? Didn't I?

NIGEL. I ain't scared of your threats no more. You ain't going to send me away. You want me to keep an eye out for you in there, man, I'll do it. I'll do it willingly too. I'll do it cause I don't want no more people dying, see. Not cause I'm scared.

You get that? Cause I don't want it. It ain't just you, you know? We don't want them people round here neither.

PHIL. 'We'?

NIGEL. Yeah, 'We'. Moslems, man. Moslems.

PHIL. You're not a Moslem, Nigel. You're a fucking spy.

NIGEL. Why can't I be a Moslem, eh? Eh? Why can't I be?

PHIL. How's your memory, Nigel?

NIGEL. What?

PHIL. Your memory? How is it? I mean, is it as drug-addled as you're making out? I put you in there, remember? Me! And just in case you don't remember who I am, I'm the guy who's quite capable of going in there, flashing my warrant card, asking everybody I meet 'Have you seen my boy Nigel? You know Nigel, don't you? He's the one who's been working undercover here for the last few weeks, taping your conversations, spying on you for the police'. And just in case you don't remember, I'm also the guy who is quite capable of breaking your neck, tossing your body in the boot of my car and driving around with it in there for a couple of weeks before I finally decide to dump it in some fucking toilet with its trousers round its ankles for the winos to piss on. How about that? Would you like that, Nigel? Would you? Who's gonna stop me, eh? Who? The police?

PHIL *has been very forceful here, knocking* NIGEL *to the ground.* NIGEL *picks himself up with a quiet dignity.*

NIGEL. You don't get it, do you? It's cause you and people like you treat people like that that kids decide they want to put off bombs. You don't leave them any fucking choice, man. You don't give folk the chance to be decent. And that's all anybody wants.

PHIL. They don't want to be decent Nigel. They want a world-wide Islamic state. They want us all to be fucking Moslems, whether we want to or not. I don't know about you, but I don't want some Mullah shoving his stone-age monkey religion down my fucking throat. I'll stand up and fight. I'd do the same if it was the fucking Christians. I'm my own man. A fucking individual. I don't need anybody telling me how to live. I don't need it, I don't want it, and I'm not fucking having it. Okay?

NIGEL. You know your trouble, Phil?

PHIL. No. Why don't you enlighten me, oh holy one?

NIGEL. You ain't got no respect, man.

PHIL. Oh yeah?

NIGEL. Yeah. You don't respect nothing. And when you don't respect nothing you don't respect yourself.

PHIL (*cupping his crotch*). Respect this, you twat.

NIGEL. See what I mean? You got no respect, man. It don't go in and it don't come out. It ain't there, man. It ain't there.

NIGEL *says this almost sorrowfully, and he says it leaving, looking back at* PHIL *with a mixture of sadness and contempt.* PHIL *is fuming.* PHIL *goes after him, manhandling him, spitting his words.*

PHIL. You'll wear that wire, Nigel. You'll wear it. You'll see. You might not care about yourself anymore, but this isn't just about you. Putting you in jail won't be the end of it. You hear me, Nigel? I'll make sure the housing association re-possess your flat. Sub-letting ain't part of your lease, is it? That old bitch'll be out on the street and the little black kid with her! What happens then, eh Nigel? Nothing good, that's for sure. And it'll all be down to you, you hear me? It'll all be your fault!

PHIL *kicks* NIGEL *as he lies on the ground.*

PHIL. Now fuck off back home! I'll be in to see you bright and early. And you better be there.

15.

NIGEL*'s flat.* MARCO *sits watching TV.* MRS MAC *is fussing around, simultaneously preparing a meal and dusting.* NIGEL *hauls his weary bones up the stairs. This latest beating has hurt. He holds his ribs from time to time. At the door he pauses. He is very aware of the choice* PHIL *has offered him – either he goes through with wearing a wire in the mosque or the law is going to come down not only on him but* MRS MAC *and* MARCO *also. He pauses outside the door, then goes in.*

MRS MAC. Hello Nigel.

NIGEL. Oh hi Mrs Mac.

MARCO. Hey, Nige.

NIGEL. Hey little buddy.

> NIGEL *takes in this scene of domestic harmony. His flat has changed of late, as has his life. Something is coming together.*

MRS MAC. Did you have a nice day, Nigel?

NIGEL. What? Oh yeah. It was okay, yeah.

MRS MAC. Now then . . .

> MRS MAC *switches channels on the TV.* MARCO *is watching.* MARCO *gives a start.*

MARCO. Hey.

> *He looks after the departing* MRS MAC, *glaring. Meanwhile* NIGEL *has picked up his book and gone to sit. He moves painfully, but tries not to let it show.*

MARCO (*whispering*). Nigel? Nigel?

NIGEL. What?

MARCO. How long's she going to be staying for?

NIGEL. What? I don't know. As long as she needs.

MARCO. But . . . Did you see that? She just . . .

NIGEL. Just leave it Marco. I mean it. I ain't in the mood, okay?

MARCO. But . . .

> NIGEL *quietens him with a look.* MRS MAC *comes through with cutlery for the meal.* NIGEL *and* MARCO *are all smiles. Until* MRS MAC *leaves.* MARCO *displays his displeasure, possibly with hand signals.*

NIGEL. Just leave it, will you.

MARCO. I just don't understand why we had to put her up.

NIGEL. She's got . . . (*Lowering voice.*) She's got no one else, okay? No one. Now leave it. I mean it.

MARCO. Okay, but do we have to have that thing sitting there?

NIGEL. What thing?

MARCO (*indicating Harry's photo*). That thing.

NIGEL. It's her husband, for fuck sake . . .

MARCO. He's ugly.

NIGEL. She's just an old lady, man. Leave her be.

MRS MAC comes through with plates of food for NIGEL and MARCO.

MRS MAC. There now. I hope you're hungry.

NIGEL. Starving.

MARCO looks disgustedly at his food. MRS MAC comes through with a plate of her own.

MRS MAC. Now then. Is it time for 'High Road'?

MARCO. No.

MRS MAC. It is so. Look. It's started.

MARCO. Nigel? (*NIGEL continues eating.*) Nigel? I am not watching that garbage again. I'm sorry, but I'm not. Ain't it bad enough we sat through it last week.

MARCO changes the channel.

NIGEL. Marco! Just leave the fucking TV alone.

NIGEL gets up and changes it back.

MRS MAC. Garbage? It most certainly is not garbage. Look at the scenery, it's lovely.

MARCO. Oh, fuck the scenery, it's crap. Look at that guy. I mean, what's he supposed to be? A block of wood? Nobody acts like that in real life.

MRS MAC. Real life? What do you know about real life? Do you think that Australian fella you idolise so much actually wrestles real crocodiles?

MARCO. Yeah. Course he does.

MRS MAC. Oh Marco, they're plastic. Anybody can see.

MARCO. They fucking are not. Nigel? Tell her? Tell her, Nigel?

NIGEL. Jesus Marco! Will you just eat your Mince and Tatties and shut the fuck up. I've had it up to here with you two bickering.

MARCO. Well they are.

It quietens down for a bit. MARCO stares daggers at MRS MAC. He mouths 'Real' at her. She mouths back 'plastic'.

NIGEL. This is really nice, Mrs Mac. Did you put something in it?

MRS MAC. Lea and Perrins. My special recipe.

NIGEL. Yeah. Thought it had a bit of a tang. Nice.

MARCO. Jesus Nigel, what planet are you on? It tastes like fucking shit, man.

NIGEL. Marco!

MARCO. It fucking does man. I thought English food was bad until I tasted Scottish food. Can't you make anything else?

MRS MAC. Of course I can. I thought you liked Mince and Tatties.

MARCO. Nobody likes Mince and Tatties.

MRS MAC. Nigel does.

MARCO. No he doesn't. He's just being polite.

MRS MAC. Well I wish you would be.

NIGEL. Oh for fuck sake, I've had enough! Either you two sort out your fucking problems or I'm fucking leaving. You can keep the flat. Cut it in half for all I care. Build a fucking fence down the middle. Do whatever it is you gotta do, but I ain't gonna be here, okay? I've had it. Had it with the both of you. Okay? Anybody wants me I'll be in my fucking room.

NIGEL*'s outburst stuns them. They sit in silence as he storms out. And storms back again.* NIGEL *picks up his Mince and Tatties, gives the pair a dirty look, and departs again.*

MRS MAC. Well, I really don't know what his problem could possibly be.

MARCO. Don't worry. He's just stressed. Super-cop's been on his back again.

MRS MAC. I never liked that one. Policeman? I thought he was a loan shark the first time I saw him.

MARCO. A loan shark. Yeah. He got that look, innit? Shifty little eyes.

MRS MAC. And a cruel mouth. Never trust a man with thin lips. Or fat ones either, come to that.

MARCO. What? You mean like mine?

MRS MAC. Oh for goodness sake, Marco, don't be stupid. You've got a lovely mouth. It's just the filth that comes out of it sometimes that bothers me. (MRS MAC *gets up.*) Here, shove up. I can hardly see the TV from there.

They watch TV together.

MARCO. You really think I've got a lovely mouth?

MRS MAC. Of course you've got a lovely mouth. You're a very handsome boy, Marco, and well you know it.

MARCO. Yeah. Yeah, I do.

MARCO *preens.*

So who's that then?

MRS MAC. That? That's Lachie, he's a crofter.

MARCO. What's that then?

MRS MAC. A crofter? Oh, I don't know. Like a farmer, only smaller. Troublemakers, usually. He's married to that one. There, talking to David Sneddon.

MARCO. Fucking hell Mrs Mac, is everybody in Scotland called David Sneddon?

MRS MAC. No, of course not.

MARCO. Well there's him, the guy from 'Fame Academy' . . .

MRS MAC. Oh Marco, why don't you do what Nigel said? Eat your Mince and Tatties and shut the fuck up.

16.

Later that night, half dark. MARCO *is in a sleeping bag in the living room.* MRS MAC *is also there, sleeping on a camp bed.* NIGEL *comes through to the kitchen area.*

MARCO. Hey Nige.

NIGEL. Hey Marco.

MARCO. You still mad?

NIGEL. What? No. I ain't mad, Marco. I just got things to deal with, you know? And you two bickering just don't help.

MARCO. Sorry.

NIGEL. S'okay.

MARCO. She's all right, that old girl, ain't she? We had a good chat last night. She ain't half as uptight as I thought she was.

NIGEL. She did your washing too. Look.

MARCO. Oh wow, that's sweet. This is okay, ain't it? Bit like having a real mum.

NIGEL. Marco, you got a real mum.

MARCO. I know, I meant a real mum, you know? Like on TV.

NIGEL. Marco man, that old bird ain't like nothing you've ever seen on TV. Look . . .

NIGEL *goes towards* MRS MAC*'s handbag.*

MARCO. You ain't gonna thieve from her?

NIGEL. No. Look.

NIGEL *manages to get* MRS MAC*'s handbag, despite her hand which moves in her sleep. He opens her bag and slowly draws out the poker she now carries everywhere with her.*

Anybody try to mug her they be sorry.

MARCO. She's game.

NIGEL. As opposed to 'On the game'.

MARCO. Ah, fuck off will you? I don't ever want to talk about that.

NIGEL. You need to see her again, Marco. You can't just blank her forever.

MARCO. Yeah I can.

NIGEL. You don't want to get bitter man. You need to let it go.

MARCO. Listen to 'Trisha'.

NIGEL. Fuck off.

MARCO. It's true. You're turning into a fucking agony aunt, man. I don't know what they're putting in the water down that fucking mosque man, but it's fucking with your head.

NIGEL. Hey, I's still Nigel from the block.

MARCO. I know. I just don't like you going there, man. I'm scared.

NIGEL. Oh . . . look . . . Come on man, come over here. I don't want to be waking Mrs Mac. (*They move to a quieter place.*)

Look . . . You got it wrong about the mosque, man. It ain't dangerous. All that shit you see on TV, that's just shit. The mosque is cool.

MARCO. What's cool about it?

NIGEL. People talk to you man, and not just about crap. They talk to you about life and stuff. Nobody's ever talked to me before, Marco. Not really talked. No fucking adult anyway. Down there though, it's different. It's like they know me or something. Like the minute I walked in that door they recognised me. There's a guy there, Ahmed, he's really funny man. Always smiling. That guy got tortured though. They took electrodes to him. They really did a job. And yet he smiling. I tell you, that Ahmed, he knows something no other grown up I've ever met knows. He just fucking knows.

MARCO. What?

NIGEL. What?

MARCO. What does he know?

NIGEL. I don't know. He ain't told me. But I know he knows, man. He's got a secret. He's an old guy and he ain't well, but he happy. Maybe that's what he knows. You can tell these guys anything, Marco. I told them about when I was little, you know, and it's like they'd heard the story before, man. Like they knew. I told them about when I was mad too. Usually, you know, usually, that's when people make their excuses, you know, usually that's when they leave. These guys, they just nod. They know the story from way back. They ain't scared. (*Pause.*) Nobody's ever talked to me before, man. Nobody.

MARCO. I talk to you.

NIGEL. Yeah, but we're mates. These guys . . . I donno . . . I don't know what it is, man. I feel better now. I feel at home. Yeah. I feel at home.

MARCO. You are at home.

NIGEL. Yeah, I know.

MRS MAC *moves in her sleep. The two wait until her breathing becomes regular again.*

MARCO. You shouldn't get too attached to those guys, Nigel.

NIGEL. What guys?

MARCO. The guys down the mosque.

NIGEL. I ain't attached to them. I likes them, that's all.

MARCO. Yeah, that's what I mean.

NIGEL. What? You think I shouldn't likes them?

MARCO. Yeah.

NIGEL. You ain't jealous are you?

MARCO. No. I ain't jealous.

NIGEL. You are, you're jealous. Aw. Don't worry, Marco. You'll still be my ichiban. You'll still be my number one bwa.

MARCO. I ain't jealous, Nigel. I'm just saying.

NIGEL. Well what you saying? I like these guys . . .

MARCO. That's it. You're spying on them, Nigel. Could be someday you gotta stand up in court.

NIGEL. I ain't going to court, man. They ain't doing nothing.

MARCO. You ain't seeing everything. Could be tomorrow one of them guys asks you to do him a favour. You ain't gonna say no, are you?

NIGEL. No.

Pause as the implications of all this sink in with NIGEL.

MARCO. I'm just saying, Nige. Hard road you're going down. Hard enough to grass up somebody you hate.

NIGEL. I ain't no grass!

MARCO. No. I know. Ain't your fault. That fucking copper man. He just ain't letting you go, is he?

MARCO *starts dragging his sleeping bag back through. He stops and looks back at* NIGEL.

I love you, Nige. You know that, don't you?

NIGEL (*lost in thought*). What? Yeah. Yeah Marco, I love you too man. I love you too.

Out on NIGEL, *thinking furiously, the reality of his new life finally sinking in.*

17.

Next morning. NIGEL *is waiting for* PHIL *to arrive. He is pretty much where we left him the night before, thinking furiously, anxious, afraid. He gets up and paces a bit. He goes to the mirror and looks himself in the eye. He looks away.*

NIGEL. Okay. Okay. Just tell him Nigel. (*He turns back to mirror.*) I ain't doing this no more, Phil. I ain't wearing your wire. (*He spins away.*) Oh fuck! I can't do this man. I can't . . . Oh shit! I'm scared.

He goes back to mirror, turns away. He wants to run. He grabs up his coat and goes to leave, but can't. He sits.

I can't do this. I can't. I can't.

PHIL *knocks on the door.* NIGEL *jumps out of his skin.*

Aaah!

NIGEL *doesn't want to answer but knows he has no choice. He goes tentatively to the door, opens it fearfully.*

PHIL *swaggers in, noticing* NIGEL's *coat and shoes are on he puts a finger on* NIGEL's *chest.*

PHIL. Going somewhere?

NIGEL. No.

PHIL. Liar.

NIGEL. I was just going to the shops, man. Honest. I'm out of smokes, man. I can't talk to people without my smokes.

PHIL *throws down a packet of cigarettes.*

PHIL. Here. Knock yourself out. (NIGEL *doesn't react.*) What's wrong?

NIGEL. Them's ready made. I roll me own.

PHIL. A smoke's a smoke, Nigel. Just take one.

NIGEL *picks up the packet and eyes it dubiously.*

What's wrong now?

NIGEL. Them things kill you man. Look, it says it here.

PHIL. Nigel? What the fuck are you talking about? You smoke thirty a day.

NIGEL. Yeah, roll-ups. Roll-ups. It's not the same thing.

PHIL. Jesus Nigel, what goes on in that head of yours? Nicotine's nicotine.

NIGEL. Ain't the nicotine that kills you man, it's these, look . . . (*He points to the contents list on the pack.*) Chemicals. Chemicals kill you, man.

PHIL. Nigel, you smoke heroin.

NIGEL. So?

PHIL. So one fucking B&H more or less isn't going to make much difference, is it? Do you want a fag or not?

NIGEL. Yeah.

Pause. NIGEL *takes a cigarette.* PHIL *gives* NIGEL *a light.*

Ain't this where you ask me if I want a blindfold?

PHIL. What?

NIGEL. Gallows' humour. Happens when I get nervous.

PHIL. What? You're not nervous are you, Nigel?

NIGEL. Kinda.

PHIL. Why? I mean, shit . . . it's only me.

NIGEL. I ain't an expert, but I was thinking the two might be connected, you know what I mean?

PHIL. Oh Nigel. Nigel, Nigel, Nigel. I'm a bit disappointed, you know? I thought by now you'd maybe got to know me a bit. I thought we'd established some kind of rapport, you know? A little trust.

NIGEL (*blowing up*). There you go again with that word, man. Why is it? Why is it? Why does that word just come slipping off your lips all the time, man. Why is it so easy for you to say?

PHIL. Nigel?

NIGEL. All you ever say to me is 'Trust me, trust me, trust me' and every time I do I just get into more and more shit. I just want to know how you do it, man? Do you just not listen to yourself or is it just that you don't mean anything you say?

PHIL. Nigel?

NIGEL. What?

PHIL. Come and sit down. There's something I need to tell you.

NIGEL. There's something I need to tell you too.

PHIL. Can't it wait?

NIGEL. No.

> NIGEL *goes to tell* PHIL *he won't do it anymore, but his courage fails. He turns away to gee himself up.*

> Okay, just say it, man. Say it. Deep breaths, say it.

PHIL. Nigel?

NIGEL. No wait, I'll say it!

PHIL. Nigel! Sit down for fuck sake!

> NIGEL *sits.*

> Okay. Look Nigel, what I've got to tell you is . . . This is never easy, so I'll just say it. Nigel . . . Karim's dead.

NIGEL. What?

PHIL. Karim's dead.

NIGEL. What?

PHIL. Your brother is dead.

NIGEL. Karim?

PHIL. Jesus Nigel, keep up to speed! Yes. Karim. Karim is dead.

NIGEL. I don't believe you? No. What? What happened?

PHIL. Why the concern? I thought you 'didn't hardly know the geezer'?

NIGEL. I didn't. But he was my brother, man. He was my brother.

> NIGEL *sits, trying to take it in. He looks at* PHIL. PHIL *shrugs and smiles.* NIGEL *is overtaken by rage and launches himself at* PHIL.

> What happened to him? Tell me? What happened to him? It was you, wasn't it? You killed him.

> PHIL *controls* NIGEL *with ease.*

PHIL. Easy Tiger. Sit down. There's something I want to show you.

> PHIL *holds* NIGEL *down as he looks around for the TV remote. He puts a video in the VCR. And switches on the TV.*

You'll like this. This is good.

He comes round behind NIGEL, *speaking beside his ear as both watch the tape.*

Now watch.

PHIL *presses play. It takes a little while for the picture to come on.*

NIGEL. Where that?

PHIL. France. Down south. Nice, eh? Look, there. That house, on the corner. Karim's in there. Now wait. Wait, wait, wait. Now! There he goes.

NIGEL. What?

PHIL. That was him, running across the road. You can't hear it cause there's no sound, but there's some French cops round that corner, just plastered the place. Wait. Yeah. Here they come.

NIGEL. Jesus.

PHIL. Yeah, impressive, aren't they? Armed police. Two little words, but to me they sound like heaven.

NIGEL. Are you stoned?

PHIL. Could be? Want some?

NIGEL. Where's Karim? Where is he, you cunt?

PHIL. Calm down, he's there, look. See the toy shop window, that shadow. Oh wait, here he comes, here he comes, out the fucking door, bang! Bang bang! Bang bang bang bang bang bang! Fucking hell. What a show.

NIGEL. They killed him.

PHIL. No.

NIGEL. They did. They fucking killed him.

PHIL. He's not dead yet. Look. See this guy. The fat one. See the way he's bending down. He's checking his pulse. Now he's looking up. He's looking at his superior. And there. See. That's where he must've done it. You've gotta fucking admire them, man. They got a wounded terrorist, mountains of paperwork, so what do they do? The fat one looks up, gestures he's still alive. Officer in charge nods his head. See. There. Fat guy takes out his gun. Puts it to his head. And . . . bang! Hmmp. Now he's dead. Now he's dead, see!

NIGEL *sits with his mouth open.* PHIL *rolls away from*
NIGEL, *intoxicated by the kill.*

I thought it was a result, you know? We're all in this together
and everything. But no. Apparently not. All I'm hearing now is
'Even the fucking French are getting results!' Everybody up to
the Home fucking Secretary, blind cunt, is shouting at me
about how even the fucking French are getting results! It's a
global operation I tell them, we're all in this together. We're all
targets so we're all victors. But no. All I hear is 'Even the
fucking French are getting results'. I tell you Nigel, to quote
Bart Simpson, 'It's a sad fucking day when I'm the voice of
reason'. Nigel? Nigel? Oh shut your mouth will you Nigel?

NIGEL. You killed him.

PHIL. Apparently not. Apparently it was the French who killed
him.

NIGEL. You fucking killed him.

PHIL. What did you expect, Nigel? It's a war. Don't you watch
the news. Hey, you should watch it tonight. Karim's on.

NIGEL. You killed him!

NIGEL *runs at* PHIL. PHIL *controls him easily, puts him in a
lazy head lock.*

PHIL. You know most days I'd punch fuck out of you for that, but
bearing in mind that I'm celebrating and you're a bit upset by
seeing your brother's brains sitting on some dusty French
sidewalk I'll give it a miss. You've got to promise though. No
more rough stuff.

NIGEL. You killed him man.

PHIL. Not me.

NIGEL. Some cunt just like you!

PHIL. He was nothing like me, Nigel. That cunt was fat. Do you
want me to wind it back?

NIGEL. No. I want you to . . . I just want you to leave man. Leave
me alone. Leave and never come back.

PHIL. Love to oblige, but apparently the word is out – If the
fucking French can do it why can't we? So, we're gonna do it,
Nigel. We're gonna get results.

NIGEL. Just leave me be.

PHIL. This is it, Nigel. One last time. I just want one more favour from you. And not for nothing. No. I'm going to pay you. How does this look? (*He holds up a really big bag of heroin.*) Oh, wait a minute. (*He opens the bag and sticks his finger in, licks his finger.*) Gotta have some perks. Shit job without them. Anyway, where was I? Oh yeah. Gotta have results.

As PHIL *says this he turns around holding a pistol in the palm of his hand. He holds it safely, unthreateningly, his finger away from the trigger, holding it up for* NIGEL *to see.* NIGEL *sees.*

NIGEL. Oh no. No.

PHIL. What?

NIGEL. No. No. Don't shoot me man.

PHIL. Oh, what? No? It's not loaded. Look.

It is loaded, and the gunshot scares them both. Both crouch down. Once the shock passes NIGEL *freaks out.*

PHIL *jumps on top of him to calm him, but* PHIL *is a bit euphoric due to the drugs he just took.*

Oh fuck, sorry Nigel. I think I killed your roof. Look. It's okay. (*He unclips the bullets.*) I'm not going to shoot you. Ssshh! It's phase two of the operation see. We're fucking up, Nigel. We've got to stop fucking up. We've been chasing terrorists for a year and a half now and all we're coming up with is zip. We've got to step up a gear. And that, my friend, is where you come in.

NIGEL. Can I have some of that heroin now please? Can I? Can I have some of that heroin now?

PHIL. Later Nige, I've just got to tell you the plan. We need to get into the mosque, see. Your little pals, they're not all they seem. But it's hard to raid a mosque see, cause it's technically a church, and it's hard to raid churches because God lives in them. Of course he doesn't. I mean if God had any sense he'd live in fucking Barbados with Sean Connery and all those other cunts, and Nigel, I think the least we can do is believe that God has sense. But no, because some fucking retards think God lives in a church we can't bust the fucking churches and we can't bust the fucking mosques, at least not without probable cause. Probable cause? Jesus. Have you ever heard such bullshit. Coppers' instinct, that's probable cause. You know, when I was a young bobby I had this commander, Bill Simmons, or was it Pete . . . Pete Simmons yeah, and he used to say . . .

NIGEL. Phil, Phil man . . . you're chuntering, man. Now normally that's pretty cool, but you've got a gun in your hand man. And that kinda scares me.

PHIL. Was I?

NIGEL. Yeah man, rabbit, rabbit, chunter, chunter . . .

PHIL *gets up off* NIGEL, *perhaps holding him down with one hand.* NIGEL *doesn't really want to get up anyway.*

PHIL. Okay. Cut to the chase, Nige. You take this gun. You put this gun in that mosque. I tell my superiors one of my informants saw a gun in the mosque. My superiors get a search warrant. We raid the place. Bad guys in jail, happy ever after.

NIGEL. But they're not bad guys.

PHIL (*shouting*). Then why do they have a gun?

NIGEL. Oh fuck man. Can we do this sometime when you're not off your face. This is terrifying me, man.

PHIL (*sitting on* NIGEL). I'm fine, Nige. Chill. It's been a good day. A long, good day.

NIGEL. Because my brother got shot.

PHIL. Basically.

NIGEL. Karim, man.

PHIL. Yeah, Karim.

PHIL *gets up.* NIGEL *gets himself together.*

NIGEL. You know the last thing he said to me?

PHIL. Nah.

NIGEL. He said – 'Who are you man? I don't know you?' I said 'It's me. Nigel. You know me.' And he said 'I don't know you. How can I know you? You dress like an American, you talk like a Jamaican, how can I know you? How can I know you if you don't know yourself?'

PHIL. Sounds like a prat.

NIGEL. Yeah. But he was my brother, man. And he was right.

PHIL. So anyway. This gun.

NIGEL. I ain't doing it man.

PHIL. I beg your pardon?

NIGEL. I ain't doing it. I ain't going to betray them.

PHIL. What do you mean, you ain't going to betray them? That's your job, Nigel. You went in there with the specific brief of getting their trust and betraying them.

NIGEL. I didn't go in there. You pushed me. You forced me in.

PHIL. You volunteered!

NIGEL. You forced me. You beat me and threatened me and pushed me. I'm weak. You knew you could get me to do anything you want. Give Nigel some drugs, he'll do it. That's what everybody says. Nigel the fuck up, Nigel the Paki. No more, man. No more. I ain't playing no more. I'm too tired.

PHIL. You're playing.

NIGEL (*looking* PHIL *in the eye*). I ain't playing, man. It's over.

PHIL. I'll kill you, Nigel. Just like they killed Karim I will kill you.

NIGEL. Yeah well. Maybe there's worse things than dying.

NIGEL *turns his back on* PHIL.

PHIL. You think?

PHIL *raises the gun slowly.*

One more chance, Nige.

NIGEL (*after the longest time, in a voice that believes he will die*). You do it.

MARCO *and* MRS MAC *come back from the shops.* MARCO *is first in the door.*

MARCO. Nigel.

PHIL *turns his head. He looks at* MARCO. MARCO *freezes.* PHIL *indicates with his gun that* MARCO *should join* NIGEL.

PHIL. You. Over there. Don't move.

He turns back to NIGEL, *not noticing* MRS MAC *as she arrives in doorway.* MRS MAC *surreptitiously opens her handbag and takes out her poker. She runs at the unfortunate* PHIL *and hits him on the head. He crumples to the ground. The gun rolls safely to his side.*

NIGEL. Fucking hell, Mrs Mac. You killed him.

MRS MAC. Oh my God! I killed him. I killed a policeman.

NIGEL. No wait, it's okay. Maybe you just stunned him.

Long pause as everybody stares at the comatose PHIL.

I saw him twitch!

MRS MAC. Where?

NIGEL. There!

MRS MAC. Oh no, he didn't. I killed him. I killed him. Oh.

NIGEL. Now you don't know that, do you? He might be alive. Marco. Marco. Take a look at him. Is he dead, man?

MARCO *comes out of his frozen state. He takes* PHIL's *pulse. He looks up at* NIGEL *holding* MRS MAC. *He looks down at* PHIL.

Is he dead?

MARCO *picks up the gun and cocks it.*

NIGEL. Marco?

MARCO. He is now.

MARCO *shoots* PHIL. MRS MAC *emits a half-choked scream.*

NIGEL. Jesus Marco, you killed him.

MARCO. Yeah. Ain't like the movies, is it Nige?

MARCO *realises what he's done. A look of fear passes across his face.*

What am I gonna do, Nigel? What am I going to do?

MARCO *starts to cry.*

NIGEL. Don't worry, man. I'll think of something.

18.

NIGEL *is being interviewed by police (tight spotlight on his face).*

NIGEL. Soup. Yeah, Campbell's cream of tomato. You know it's 'ad its picture painted? I am telling you. That's what I was doing man. That's exactly what I was doing when he came busting in. Officer Phil. Yeah. The deceased. I don't know, officer, he came pushing in accusing me of all sorts. Seems he thought I was some kind of gangster or something. Why ain't that credible? Yeah, well, maybe you's right, maybe I is the world's biggest fuck up, but he's still standing there accusing me of all sorts. I told him. Course I did. He just wouldn't listen. Kept coming back and coming back. You did this, you did that. I was shitting it, couldn't work out why this cop won't leave me alone. Then one day I realise. Yeah, then one day I realise. Look, could you turn that tape off now? I know that but I don't really want to talk about this. It was really quite traumatic what he did. I'm trying officer, but sometimes when I close my eyes I can still feel that hard manly stubble and smell the sweet smell of Brut. Yeah I's saying he forced his self on me. You think I want to do that stuff? I ain't like that, man. Or at least I wasn't. Not until I met Officer Phil. I don't know, officer, maybe he sensed something in me. I ain't had a girlfriend well since never and after he'd done it, I don't know . . . just felt nice, you know, lying there in his arms, felt safe. An' besides. He was giving me drugs by then so I was like thinking, okay, maybe that hurt a bit but fair trade ain't no robbery. I'm sorry, what does 'amoral' mean? Ah. Well back then maybe, but I've got religion now. Oh yeah, he came back. He always came back. Ask Mrs Mac. She me neighbour.

Spotlight switches to MRS MAC.

MRS MAC. Oh yes, I saw him there loads of times. I thought he was a debt collector if you can believe that. In fact I told him, Nigel's so feckless you know, he wouldn't be able to pay off a loan. He's only got his disability money. He's not right in the head you know. Away with the fairies if you'll pardon the pun. Yes, well, I thought he was getting beaten up, all the shouting and banging, the groans I could hear. But then the young man told me he was a policeman, so I had to assume that everything was above board.

Little did I know.

Spotlight switches back to NIGEL.

NIGEL. I knew he was abusing me, but I quite liked it see. It was only when Marco came on the scene that things went a bit scue-wiff. I never knew Marco was gay or nothing. I thought he was just the kid up the stairs. I found him one day just bleeding all over the place, crying his little heart out . . . Yes, he had been, and you know who did it? His fucking mother man. Pardon my language, but that slut was hitting him with a coat hanger. Couldn't just leave him like that, could I? He's just a kid, man. Yeah, he live with me now. I invite him back for a bit. I thought it would be okay, but officer Phil, man, he

get so cross, so cross man. He said he knew I was two timing
him and he'd get even. He said he was gonna plant some drugs
on me and arrest me himself. He said everybody in jail would
have my bum, not just him. But I couldn't help it. I was falling
in love with Marco. Have you ever been in love, officer? I got
to tell you they is right, it is the sweetest feeling. Yeah, I know
he just fifteen, but that ain't no problem if we never have sex.
To tell you the truth officer, after what that filthy Phil put me
through, I don't know if I ever have any sex again. He used to
take his gun to bed with him, you know? 'Call me Clint', that's
what he whisper. Yeah, I know that now, very unusual and
probably illegal, but what did I know? I thought maybe that
was just normal, you know? I ain't never done that sort of thing
before. Forgive my language again officer, but that was one
fucked-up dude you had working for you there.

Spotlight switches to MRS MAC.

MRS MAC. I just came back with the shopping. Nigel's been
letting me stay while my flat gets renovated. Yes, it was very
unfortunate. I'm going electric from here on in. Anyway. I just
came home with my shopping and there he was. He had his
gun in his hand and he was waving it about like a madman. I
think he was on drugs, you know? Shouldn't be surprised. He
was shouting, 'Him or me, make up your mind' and poor
Nigel, he was hiding behind the sofa whimpering 'Don't kill
me, don't kill me, I's too young to die'. And that was when I
went for him.

Spotlight switches to NIGEL.

NIGEL. Oh yeah, she went for him.

Spotlight switches to MRS MAC.

MRS MAC. I went for him. I picked up the poker and hit him on
the head. I thought I'd killed him. I was traumatised. But
Nigel's been so good to me, you see, and that monster . . .
I saw red, you see. I quite literally saw red.

Spotlight switches to NIGEL.

NIGEL. I thought he was going to kill me. But Mrs Mac saved the
day. She charge in with that metal stick and crack him one, just
crack him! I owe my life to that plucky Scottish grandmother.

Spotlight switches to MRS MAC.

MRS MAC. I thought I'd killed him. I'd never killed anyone
before. All these tears welled up, and I just cried. But he wasn't

dead, you see. It was like those awful movies when the monster never dies. He had the gun. He came alive. He turned to Nigel. I thought he was going to shoot. But then he took the gun . . .

Spotlight switches to NIGEL.

NIGEL. An' he puts it in his mouth. He puts it in his mouth right, and . . . boom! Bye bye Phil, man. Fucking Bye bye Phil. (*Pause, a traumatised* NIGEL *rests his weary head on his hand.*) Is you guys gonna pay for my carpet by the way?

Spotlight switches to MRS MAC.

MRS MAC. It was quite a night, all in all.

Spotlight switches to MARCO.

MARCO. I ain't no batty boy, who told you that? Well Nigel's got the wrong end of the stick then. Me and him's gonna have some serious words, I can tell you. No, I told you, I was at the football when it happened. I was somewhere else.

19.

NIGEL*'s flat.* NIGEL, MARCO *and* MRS MAC *sit around, a picture of domestic bliss, a family.* MRS MAC *is knitting.* MARCO *is eating from a big bag of crisps.* NIGEL *look up from his book.*

NIGEL. You all right there, Mrs Mac?

MRS MAC. I'm fine, Nigel.

NIGEL. How about you Marco? You all right?

MARCO. I'm fine, Nigel, thanks.

NIGEL. Good. Want to watch some TV?

MARCO. Yeah, why not?

MARCO *switches on the TV. It is the news.*

NEWSREADER. Today Tony Blair flew to the Azores for a meeting which ministers maintain is a final bid for peace but many see as a council of war. Troops in the Gulf are already on high alert, and many fear that war now is both inevitable and imminent, with predictions that coalition planes could mount a first strike as early as Thursday.

MRS MAC. Oh, that's so depressing. Is there nothing else on?

MARCO *switches channels. It is 'Only Fools and Horses'.*

NIGEL. Oh, I love this guy.

He bounds across to the sofa.

Shove up.

They watch the show, digging into the crisps, their faces alternately blank and eager, innocent and blissful.

'You plonker, Rodney'. 'Cushti'.

Out on their faces in the blue light of the TV, while MRS MAC *looks across, content.*

A Nick Hern Book

The People Next Door first published in Great Britain in 2003
as a paperback original by Nick Hern Books Limited,
14 Larden Road, London W3 7ST, in association with
the Traverse Theatre, Edinburgh

The People Next Door copyright © 2003 Henry Adam

Henry Adam has asserted his right to be identified
as the author of this work

Typeset by Country Setting, Kingsdown, Kent CT14 8ES

Printed and bound in Great Britain by Bookmarque,
Croydon, Surrey

ISBN 1 85459 767 1

A CIP catalogue record for this book is available
rom the British Library